D0105334

Competency Based
Teacher Education

Dan W. Andersen

James M. Cooper

M. Vere DeVault

George E. Dickson

Charles E. Johnson

Wilford A. Weber

McCutchan Publishing Corporation
2526 Grove Street
Berkeley, California 94704

This work was developed under a grant from the U.S. Office of
Education, Department of Health, Education, and Welfare. However,
the opinions and other content do not necessarily reflect the position
or policy of the Agency, and no official endorsement should be
inferred.

Contents

Book Two: A Systems Approach to Program Design

Competency Based

Teacher Education: 1

Problems and Prospects for the Decades Ahead

M. Vere DeVault
Dan W. Andersen
George E. Dickson

McCutchan Publishing Corporation
2526 Grove Street
Berkeley, California 94704

Contents

Foreword

Within the past several years, the movement toward competency based teacher education programs has accelerated at a striking rate. In its simplest form, a competency based program may be defined as one that specifies the objectives for training of teachers in an explicit form, and then proceeds to hold the prospective teachers accountable for meeting those objectives. Such a program, however, demands two major technologies that only recently became available to teacher education.

The first of these is a systems design that permits the employment of a sophisticated management schema. Only through such a management plan can the program really be controlled, evaluated, and renewed. The second technology is the modularization of the instructional program. The individualization of the program has been made possible through the development of learning modules whose use permits self-pacing by the students and instructors.

The availability of these technologies to teacher education has been hastened by the Elementary Teacher Education Models Program supported over the past several years by the Office of Education. The products of that program, frequently referred to as Models of Teacher Education, have had a significant impact on American education, particularly through their application of systematic research and program development to the training of teachers. This application now undergirds the national movement toward performance based programs. It is, indeed, a fundamental prerequisite to the success of the competency based program.

During the course of the models program, eight of the project directors most closely associated with it came to appreciate the value of joint exploration of the problems and prospects of teacher education. They began to hold regular meetings across the nation to explore their common concerns and exchange ideas. This text addresses the major issues that we have debated on the platforms of state and national meetings for two years as well as with our colleagues in our school and university communities.

The conflicts between systems designs and personalization of instruction must be resolved. Continuity in teacher education is essential both in sequence (preservice through inservice) and through interdisciplinary curricula. The determination of the role of technology in the maintenance and enhancement of human values is a crucial need for the 1970s. The changing role of the student in relation to the university must be considered. Changing faculty roles and the multi-institutional support necessary must emerge as effective instruments in the preparation of teachers.

After these two years of discussion with colleages at universities, schools, state departments of education, the Office of Education, students, parents, and teachers, the debate continues. The ideas of individuals and of the group continue to evolve. Yet, it seemed important to fix on a point in time to publish the consensus of the group and share with the profession the ideas and questions that had been generated during four years of effort. This text addresses those major issues that seem essential to the implementation of a competency based teacher education program. Although individual chapters were the responsibility of the authors indicated, early drafts of each chapter were evolved through vigorous debate in a succession of meetings over a two-year period.

James P. Steffensen
Office of Education

Preface

The models were initially specified by large numbers of faculty members on each of the campuses represented by the authors. We recognize our indebtedness to those unnamed colleagues whose contributions are more specifically recognized in the several reports from each of the models projects.

Dissemination efforts have put the authors in touch with college, university, and public school faculties both in sharing ideas and in efforts to implement aspects of competency based teacher education. We recognize that we have learned a great deal in this process from those with whom we were sharing ideas. Specifically, we are indebted to those directors and faculty members of the Consortium of Southern Colleges for Teacher Education, with whom we have had national conferences and many intercampus meetings. Their contributions, through debate, pilot implementation, and reactions to an early draft of this manuscript have been invaluable, and their continuing exchange of ideas will be warmly remembered by all of us as among our most useful and enjoyable professional experiences. The directors include Pearlie Dove, Clark College; Willie Everett Combs, Florida A & M University; Edward C. Powell, Jarvis Christian College; Howard Fortnoy, Livingston University; M. Sharif Hafiz, Norfolk State College; Norman C. Johnson, North Carolina Central University; N. M. McMillan, Shaw University; Isaac Bracey, South Carolina State College; Dorothy Draper, Tennessee State University; and Argiro L. Morgan, Xavier University.

Special mention must be given to the Office of Education personnel who, in a variety of ways more important than initial or continued funding, contributed to our critical examination of the issues. The challenge of the leadership in the Bureau of Educational Personnel Development, and especially in the Teacher Corps, has provided a vehicle for the practical test of many of the ideas explored here.

More specifically, we recognize with much appreciation the initial and continuing support of three members of the National Center for Educational Research and Development (NCERD). Glen Boerrigter initiated the program and has continued to support our efforts over a period of several years. James Steffensen, program director, has been a source of continuing inspiration and support. We also express our sincere appreciation to Shirley Steele of NCERD for her sensitive professional assistance at every turn.

Contributors

Dan W. Andersen, Professor, Department of Curriculum and Instruction, University of Wisconsin, Madison, Wisconsin.

J. Bruce Burke, Director, The Humanities Teaching Institute, Michigan State University, East Lansing, Michigan.

Richard T. Coffing, Associate Professor, School of Education, University of Massachusetts, Amherst, Massachusetts.

James M. Cooper, Associate Dean, College of Education, University of Houston, Houston, Texas.

M. Vere DeVault, Professor, Department of Curriculum and Instruction, University of Wisconsin, Madison, Wisconsin.

Walter Dick, Assistant Dean, Research and Development, College of Education, Florida State University, Tallahassee, Florida.

George E. Dickson, Dean, College of Education, University of Toledo, Toledo, Ohio.

Norman R. Dodl, Associate Professor, Department of Elementary Education, Florida State University, Tallahassee, Florida.

Jesse Garrison, Professor, Oregon College of Education, Monmouth, Oregon.

W. Robert Houston, Professor, College of Education, University of Houston, Houston, Texas.

Charles E. Johnson, Professor, College of Education, University of Georgia, Athens, Georgia.

John M. Kean, Associate Professor, Department of Curriculum and Instruction, University of Wisconsin, Madison, Wisconsin.

Walt Le Baron, Consultant, Washington, D.C.

H. Del Schalock, Research Professor, Oregon College of Education, Monmouth, Oregon.

Wilford A. Weber, Associate Professor, College of Education, University of Houston, Houston, Texas.

William Wiersma, Jr., Professor, College of Education, University of Toledo, Toledo, Ohio.

1
Relevance and Teacher Education

George E. Dickson
John M. Kean
Dan W. Andersen

Position

Teachers of the young share a large part of the responsibility for determining the future of mankind. Both parents and society have put in their charge the nurturing of the intellect and ultimately the preparation of children to improve mankind's position on this earth. The importance of the education of teachers cannot be overemphasized. As Whitehead aptly states, "education's successful accomplishment depends on a delicate adjustment of many variable factors [because] ... we are dealing with human minds ..."[1] The task of those responsible for teacher education is to prepare teachers able to orchestrate these variables so that children learn what best prepares them to improve mankind's relation to the world. Relevance requires that we continuously assess the relationship between teachers' education and their ultimate functioning as teachers. When we say those responsible for educating teachers, we mean everyone from the kindergarten teacher to the college president.

Rationale

To talk about relevance we must talk about the conditions under which we can claim relevance: conditions that allow us to retain control over our own participation in the world's affairs. The following assertions identify conditions essential to maintain relevance:

1. We must contribute to the solution of societal problems. Teacher education exists in a political society; a technological society; an alienated society; a society that needs leaders, people who can communicate, people skilled in the humane use of resources, and people who are capable of controlling and changing the conditions of society to help it meet its needs.

2. Our programs must continually reflect the real world. We must build into our programs the opportunity and space to promote regeneration to meet the changing conditions of the world. In essence, we must be able to change our own interaction with students as change results from new infusions of knowledge from research, widened perspectives on man's relationship to man, or the vagaries of the human condition: war and peace, the environment, human communication, human sexual nature, crime, poverty, or less obvious complicating factors.

3. We must understand and satisfy the needs of our students as both we and they perceive them. The best learning is that learned at one's own behest, but this truism does not suggest everything to be learned is introduced after a need is perceived. As teacher educators it is our function to help teachers perceive their needs and theirs to help us perceive and fulfill them.

4. We must live our lives as we teach. Students rightly suspect, in Arrowsmith's words, "a fatal hypocrisy in the teacher who lives without the slightest relation to what he knows, whose texts are wholly divorced from his life, from human life." [2]

5. Our theoretical ideas must find important applications within our students' curricula. Today, "We must educate so people can cope efficiently, imaginatively, and perceptively with information overload." [3] Our management sciences, our technological proficiency, and our concern for human welfare enable us to begin a transformation of teacher education that will bring practice into line with theory.

In one sense, this entire book is about how to make ourselves and our programs relevant. It suggests the conditions and procedures that reflect our thinking about the changing nature of education in a changing society. We are stating both what teacher education ought to become and what it must become.

Where does teacher education stand in this context? Teachers' attitudes and actions are undergoing considerable change. They are becoming more political and less quiescent. They show signs of restiveness; they are not and will not be unresponsive to societal concerns.

The voice of youth, the state of society, and the possible form of the future all indicate flaws in present conditions. Teacher education as usual or the promotion of piecemeal innovative efforts dealing with isolated issues is inadequate. New responses are required to the new products, processes, and social needs resulting from the ramifications of technology in a changing society.

Problems of Society

To whom or to what is teacher education to be relevant? Presumably we are helping others learn to teach children so they can survive with grace and personal fulfillment in a society that cannot always define its wants for itself and its youth. Schooling is one of the primary means of initiating children into the world. From the old deluder Satan laws of Massachusetts to the National Defense loans of the early sixties we have been extremely conscious of the need to fit youth into society while protecting the already initiated members and to protect children and youth from learning too many of their lessons from the hard taskmaster, experience. However selfish our motives might be, they stem from our interest in the collective good.

To begin analyzing our responsibility, we must reexamine the major social forces confronting education and particularly teacher education. Grambs has rightly accused us, and the whole of higher education, of not considering "(1) the uncertain state of international balance, (2) the dislocations [both personal and social] of technology, and, (3) the divergent views of the role of education and possible solutions to the problems of educational practice."[4] We need teacher educators who are more responsive to these factors if we are going to be relevant now and in the uncertain future.

Democratic Ideals and Social Reality

The democratic ideals extolled by the United States are being seriously challenged by friendly nations and responsible persons. The operational meaning of democracy abroad is widely questioned, and this questioning has not been lost upon American youth. They protest against leaders whom they see acting undemocratically;

they know that wars have not made "the world safe for democracy"; they wonder at the apparent shallowness and emptiness of a democratic society that has an almost fanatical attitude about its "defense," which needs constant, undeclared wars in faraway places to protect it from communism; they understand the power of the military-industrial complex, the money demanded by it, and the money made from it; and they increasingly wonder whether they can work within our democratic system to secure peace and happiness for all mankind.

It seems that our stated commitment to academic goals and our teachings about pluralism in society have not permeated the lives of students to any great extent. We have implied that one can conceptualize education's ends without dealing with its political constraints. Our own ignorance about political ideology, economics, and even different religions has left us without the intellectual armor to rethink our curriculum and has made us blind to possibilities that exist for organizing curriculum around communication, war, economics, or any other major factor that must be understood if we are to work for peace among all peoples.

The basic reorganization of teacher education will force the public specification of goals and criteria and will open our programs to examination for discrepancies between rhetoric and practice. Too many teachers even now fear talking about both the right and the left, political balance, the United Nations, communism, socialism, Buddhism, contrasts between cultures, and even drugs. Our schools may lead, may reflect and respond, or may follow far behind society as we struggle to form a better world. If we are to begin we must clarify what we hope to do.

Dislocations Resulting from Technology

Technological changes in our society have introduced profound personal and social adjustments and displacements. Migration from farms (especially those located in the rural south) to the city is a result of technological change; less manpower is needed on farms and more is needed in urban industrial locations. The problems caused by this population shift are well documented. Thousands of people with inappropriate skills and education enter an environment with very different demands from the one they left; the results are urban ghettos, unemployment, and expansion of the other symptoms of societal "sickness." The demands for unskilled labor have decreased with the increasing mechanization of both heavy and light industry and of service occupations. As the unskilled have been displaced by technology, they have not been given enough opportunities to enter new job markets (construction trades, for example), or to develop skills for more technical positions. As society in general has become more affluent, the economic and social squeeze on the lowest levels of society has increased.

Teachers and teacher educators have never claimed to prepare children for unskilled jobs. We have tended to respond to technology after the fact; we have not really faced the implications of technology with any kind of rational policy to help people change their work orientation. A new focus is imperative. Children need new models to cope with the problems of technology; they must anticipate new alternatives.

Divergent Views of the Role of Education

Out traditional commitment to academic goals has had little influence on the lives of most students. Education for participation in a democracy is a basic goal in America; no other country has educated so many through so long a period of schooling. Why such an abundance of schooling? What has it done for the young? What should it do? The answer at the moment appears to be education for vocational proficiency. Students are prepared to serve effectively in specially identified social roles; scientific and technical needs have high priority.

The confusion about the proper content of education shows that educational critics are far apart. Some wish schools to develop an intellectual elite by transmitting the heritage of great ideas to emerging generations with suitable academic rigor. Some want schools to free children, reward diversity, and encourage creativity. Some want education to give power to people, or equip them to reorganize society. The critics agree on only two things: the schools and universities have not done the job hoped for, and something must be done.

As our citizens become exposed to more education, they become less satisfied with the accomplishments of the schools. This conflict on the aims of education must be resolved, because it is a deterrent to effective education and poses a continuous dilemma in the education of teachers. The educational establishment resists change; determining the role of education and making necessary modifications will not be an easy task. We agree with Shields that

responsible use could be most appropriately defined for now at least as rais-
ing the sensibilities of a wide range of the population to the realities of our
American educational system in terms of a more humanized vision of a man's
place in the universe than the one that has emerged in our highly industrialized,
militarized, and centralized world. There has been enough experience with reform and reform-failure to give credibility to the belief of the young revolu-
tionaries that this kind of sensibility on a wide scale is the *sine qua non* for a
significant qualitative as well as quantitative change in American education.[5]

In the past we have tended to talk as if the school had only one role, which was the same regardless of where one went. We have simply assumed that a teacher educated in Whitewater, Wisconsin is prepared to teach in San Francisco. As more people examine alternatives to the uniform-school idea, we begin to recognize the need to prepare teachers for greater tolerance and flexibility. The cultural differences among citizens, which are only now being both recognized and respected, will result in different demands on teachers.

Schools must identify and adapt to important social and cultural factors that are changing peoples' lives. Pressures from such change factors are too powerful to be held in abeyance, and the educational system must find ways to accommodate them even as students in the schools must be taught to understand and cope with them.

Congruence with the Real World

What has been the response of the teacher educators to these problems? We have remained devoted principally to teaching reading, writing, and arithmetic; we have decorously abstained from dealing with either the political problems of the world or the social problems at home. In general we have not helped schools organize their teaching around politics, environment, or communication. To take a specific example, the schools have seldom served the residents of our inner cities as a springboard to escape poverty. Schools, as they are typically constituted and operated, have not provided the hoped for payoff for disadvantaged youth. It is no wonder the inner city youth has become alienated from the school. School has become not a place to succeed but a place to fail. The sorting and grading system practiced by the schools usually rewards affluent children and handicaps the less than affluent. Although we know success builds success and failure is self-replicating, few attempts are made to interrupt the failure cycle. Youth are not only alienated from school; they also reject the "system" that produced it. Of course, most young people work within the system, but since this is the line of least resistance, we should not be encouraged by it.

Teacher education is especially vulnerable to criticism because it is geared to help others solve problems, not to deal with them directly. Besides this, we have not yet asked serious questions about how to foster learning in college, university, and school communities we do influence directly. We have at times put off our students with pleas for patience, hoping that as we make progress they will come to understand how a teacher conducts himself. We have let ourselves believe a host of myths about preservice and inservice education. Students' experiences with preservice and inservice education have neither increased their abilities to deal with change or atypical problems, nor stimulated them to improve their relationships with children and their communities.

Our situation demands that *all* personnel involved in the educational enterprise be given adequate and appropriate reeducation, or the changes we make will be negligible. Public school personnel, as well as college and university personnel, will need specific instructional experiences to bring their knowledge and abilities up to date and make them consistent with current developments and reform. Education must be a continuing process for all who are involved with teacher training. Instructional targets must include not only preservice but also inservice and other populations. Only then will teacher education's effects be felt on a wide enough scale to cause real change.

Needs of Students

The learner's needs, interests, and perceptions must increasingly determine the function of the teacher in each learning situation. In the past the teacher's task was shaped primarily by his subject matter or by standard educational goals. As educators face the need to identify relevant education for individual students, for diverse groups, and for various age levels, the tasks of the teacher will be derived increasingly from the nature of the learner.

Student Participation

Students are demanding a voice not only in determining the nature of curriculum within courses and within schools, but also in choosing their own educational objectives. As Rossman suggests, only the satisfaction of these demands will make student participation relevant. "It seems more useful to configure the roles of expert, teacher, and pupil back into a single field and try to understand what does or should go on in the field in which the learner is embedded."[6] If students are to select options effectively and determine their own curriculum, they must be offered experiences that help them determine what is relevant to their goals. This will result in continuous interaction between practice in the schools and theory on campus.

Live as We Teach

To live as we teach requires staff members to involve themselves actively with students in the learning process. Michael has emphasized that it will become increasingly impossible for us to develop any kind of rapport with students if we maintain a neutral stance before our students. "Indeed, a neutral teacher can only diseducate the student about his coming world of turmoil, conflict, and confusion. To be of it (the world) as citizen or leader will require commitment and the will and courage to trust, to experiment and to live with crises of conscience."[7]

Too often in the past college age youth could not see in our rhetoric, our programs, and presumably our personal lives evidence that human beings were our central concern. We cannot say that people are at the heart of all teacher education programs and act otherwise in our interaction with teachers. We must show our feelings and opinions; we cannot hide behind authoritarian dispassion.

Innovative teacher education represents only the beginning of a completely reformed institution within which each person can learn in his own unique way. We need a systematic organization of the goals, content, and processes of education to make obsolete the necessity of dealing with people primarily as a herd. We no longer want to depend on the lecture as the vehicle for dealing with our students. Technological tools now being developed can handle the tremendous amount of information relating both to student progress and subject matter. As we develop approaches to restructure teacher education, these same approaches can restructure public schools. We must begin to teach in the way we want others to teach. We must model the processes we talk about.

Theory and Application

Teacher education will have to be in the vanguard of experimental learning programs. We do not want to be in the position of the minister who counsels teetotaling and gets drunk regularly, the family counselor who winds up in a divorce court, or the physician who neglects his own health. We must apply our theory to ourselves.

Role of Research

The time has come for teacher educators, teachers, and preservice teachers to seek and use research findings on teacher behavior and characteristics, to become adept in assessing and evaluating teacher behavior and style, and to employ research as a basic part of the teaching process.

We must prepare teachers who are ready, willing, and able to do their own clinical research. Such teachers will view teaching not as a craft where traditional rules are applied but as an art where the individual is continually seeking new solutions. Each teacher should be equipped to find out for himself which behaviors are most comfortable for his personality and most effective in his situation. This calls for teachers with an experimental attitude, theoretical knowledge of past research and experience, technical skills to control the media of instruction, and knowledge of evaluation techniques to analyze feedback on educational objectives. We need a research strategy different from that of the past. As Medley clearly puts it:

> It appears that research, evaluation, and what might be called the teacher's own clinical experience, can all merge into a single operation which has the potential of achieving the functions of all three—development of research knowledge, provision of continuous diagnostic feedback to the program, and facilitation of teacher self-improvement at both the pre-service and in-service levels— much more effectively than any present structure does or could possibly do.[8]

Disciplines

Relevance in teacher education will be enhanced as the boundaries between disciplines disappear. The distinction between content and methods, psychology and instruction, and curriculum and foundations must not be allowed to overshadow their interdependence. Disciplines will form new configurations relevant to teacher education's new needs.

Diversity in Programing

Teacher education demands new diversity. Accrediting associations and certification regulations contribute to the conformity that institutions enforce in program planning and instructional procedure. The needs of individual students will be met more readily when diversity among teacher education programs provides a wide variety of learning patterns. Enrollment in a particular institution should indicate the student's personal orientation and to some extent his future professional outlook. The conflict between the need for minimum standards and the need for flexibility can be resolved by cooperation among teacher education programs, state departments of education, and schools. Traditional forms of certification will not disappear, because not all institutions will choose performance based, systems developed models. However, the existence of such models will enable people to work without being confined by traditional standards.

Instructional Process

A complete reevaluation of the instructional process is under way and will continue. It is the process itself, rather than the traditional concept of learning as a product, that will determine the nature of instruction in the decades ahead. The planning and instruction necessary for one-to-one, small group, class-size group, large group, and independent study activities requires an elementary school organization that facilitates team teaching.

Preparing teachers for the future will require more efficient use of their abilities and efforts. The elementary teacher needs more specialized training. Each teacher should be competent in a specific subject such as language arts, reading, mathematics, social studies, or science, beyond his general competence in other subjects. The differentiated staff concept will permit wider use of teaching specialists; such use provides children with more competent teaching in each field.

Consequences of Relevance

Teaching tasks must change and teacher educators must take cognizance of social change and contemporary developments. Teacher education has not kept pace with today's schools, and the gap between present requirements and existing programs continues to increase. In the final third of the twentieth century teacher training must be mutable: it must not only be relevant to existing conditions; it must also be adaptable to unforeseeable future ones.

In the past teacher education has suffered from tremendous pressure to conform to the established disciplines. Thus it has been an imitator rather than an innovator. This stance has served neither the interests of teacher education nor those of society. We have left ourselves open to charges like the following:

> It will be argued that we have teacher-training institutes with all kinds of courses in all areas of education. But this is self-delusion. What our teachers colleges do is something badly needed and useful; but it is not to teach anyone how to teach. They are recruiting agencies. They procure potential teachers and give them a seal of approval that guarantees their employment and entitles them to tenure. It also gives them self-confidence, and this is no small thing. But beyond that it is hard to see what the seventeen-year-old high school girl of yesterday did not know or do when she started to teach elementary school in the rural midwest.[9]

We can defend ourselves by replying, "A revolution is underway in the education of teachers. The path to the teaching profession is changing as dramatically as the path to the medical profession changed following the historic Flexner Report of medical education in 1910."[10] Teacher educators must both react to change and anticipate it. They must make teachers aware of the pressures they are likely to encounter, the probable future consequences of their influence on children, and the techniques and tools they can choose from to develop alternate teaching strategies.

Professionalism

Professional education must assume responsibility for its own standards, development, and priorities. The accrediting of institutions for the preparation and certification of teachers must be in the hands of the education profession. Progressive educational reform and development can be fostered only by a profession fully aware of the needs of society and the contribution it can make in meeting those needs.

Change in the Schools

If new teacher education programs are to be developed for the challenging future, corresponding innovations must be made in the school settings both where the programs are to be applied and where their products are placed. Teacher education planners—both school and university personnel—must first assume that it is impracticable to prepare teachers for the outmoded schools of the past. The primary function of the elementary school of the future is to develop a viable program of individually guided education. This goal cannot be carried out without an adequate supply of personnel, from teaching team leaders to paraprofessionals. Schools must be organized to permit such staffing.

At this point we might ask where the basic changes in education have originated in our recent past. They have rarely come from educators. The two sources that appear to have been the most productive and influential are (1) federal programs, such as Teacher Corps, Head Start, Upward Bound, Title III of the Elementary and Secondary Education Act, Job Corps; and (2) new educational technology, such as programed instruction, computers, overhead projectors, 8 mm film loops, electrostatic duplicators, tape recorders, and paperbacks. These factors are making it impossible to delay restructuring teacher preparation for the changing role of education. In the decades ahead, education will serve society best by serving the individual first; we must strike a balance between the needs of both society and the individual. By the 1990s education must accommodate to both humanistic and technological requirements. In our struggle to remain relevant we must face questions we cannot answer now. Will our programs resolve dissent? Can we help solve the problems society faces today? Can we change the image of teacher education in the eyes of prospective teachers, our colleagues, and the public? Can we really provide the help that ghetto parents are demanding? Can teacher education discover and respond to the true needs of society? We will not know until we try.

Teacher educators are charged with seeking or creating environments in which they and their students can explore, criticize, preserve, and transmit knowledge and values to improve the quality of life. We do not single out faculty as opposed to students or graduate students as opposed to undergraduates. The responsibility does not rest with deans or departmental chairmen only; we are all charged with it, both now and in the future.

Footnotes

1. Alfred North Whitehead, *The Aims of Education* (New York: Macmillan, Mentor Books, 1929), p. 17.

2. William Arrowsmith, "The Future of Teaching," in *Campus 1980*, ed. Alvin C. Eurich (New York: Delacorte Press, 1968), p. 120.

3. Donald N. Michael, *The Unprepared Society: Planning for a Precarious Future* (New York: Basic Books, 1968), p. 108.

4. Jean D. Grambs, "Social Influences on Education," in *Educational Comment 1969* (Toledo, Ohio: University of Toledo), p. 114.

5. James J. Shields, Jr., "Foundations of Education: Relevance Redefined," *The Record* 71 (December 1969): 198.

6. Michael Rossman, "Learning and Social Change: The Problem of Authority," in *The Changing College Classroom*, ed. Phillip Runkel et al. (San Francisco: Jossey-Bass, 1969), p. 28.

7. Michael, *The Unprepared Society*, p. 120.

8. Donald M. Medley, "The Research Context and the Goals of Teacher Education," in *Educational Comment 1969: Contexts for Teacher Education* (Toledo, Ohio: University of Toledo), p. 131.

9. Peter F. Drucker, *The Age of Discontinuity: Guidelines to Our Changing Society,* (New York: Harper & Row, 1969), p. 338.

10. *The New Teacher: A Report on Ford Foundation Assistance for New Patterns with the Education of Teachers* (New York, Ford Foundation, 1962).

2
Systems Analysis and Teacher Education

Walt Le Baron

Position

Changing demands of society, increasingly complex technologies, and variable economic support levels necessitate more deliberate planning for education. Systems analysis offers goal oriented procedures to effect this deliberate planning.

Rationale

Four major emphases have emerged in the development of systems planning for teacher education:

1. The teacher's role is designed, and teacher education is developed, in the context of the related roles of aides, educational technologists, and curriculum and supervisory personnel.

2. The teacher's role is designed in relation to all the elements of the learning environment: books, theories of teaching, machines, curriculum.

3. The distinction between preservice and inservice training has decreased as teaching is viewed as a continuing developmental process.

4. Therefore, teacher education has become goal oriented, i.e., based on the development of the competencies teachers need to

facilitate children's learning. This chapter will explore the basic ideas of systems analysis and the contributions it could make in the development of teacher education programs.

Systems Analysis

Systems analysis is a general term for the application of scientific thinking to large-scale problems. The phrase has been used indiscriminately to mean the analysis of information for computer programing, the development of planned management activities, or simply the orderly relation of two or more things to ideas.

There is no single method of systems analysis, and it is not solely the product of our computer age; indeed, its history in one sense goes back at least to Aristotle. What is new is a concentration on the quantifiable aspects of analysis (to the extent that this is possible) and on the isolation and control of numerous variables made possible by computers. This has led to a revolution in our thinking about the nature, organization, and use of information, so that at the heart of systems procedures there now exists a philosophy of information.

The word *system* communicates many different ideas, but in the present context it indicates a concentration on process. In briefest form, then, by *systems analysis* I mean an orderly process for (1) defining and describing a universe of interest and the significant factors and their interrelationships within that universe, and (2) determining what changes in the universe will cause a desired effect. Beginning with the broadest statement of the universe, these procedures permit the analyst to isolate and define parts of the system according to their functions and then to note the interrelationships among these functions.

The developers of the elementary teacher education models have found several different approaches suitable to the use of systems theory. One approach might be selected over others because it appears to be most promising in terms of problem analysis, for example, but all the approaches concentrate on process and function.

Designing the System

Six basic steps seem useful for developing some ideas about

systems analysis. Figure 1 shows these steps and suggests the basic feedback relationships among them.

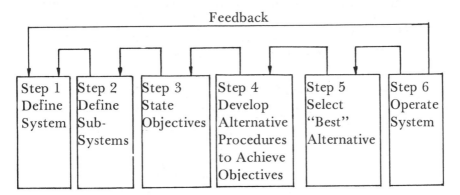

Fig. 1. Steps in systems analysis

The term *reiteration* describes a significant aspect of systems analysis. The system designers begin by working through all the steps (except operation) at a general level and then returning to the beginning to develop details based on the knowledge of this overview. Through a continuing process each step becomes more finely detailed, hence more clearly developed. By beginning with the most general overview and working through to the details, each specific action can be related to the major goals of the project and evaluated on that basis. In the design of teacher education programs, this principle requires beginning with a description of the total educational program and its institutions, and then determining the role or roles of the teachers in the program. Eventually, the specific teacher competencies would be described, along with programs for their development.

Implementing the System

Assuming that sufficient resources are available, systems implementation should be relatively automatic if the system has been carefully designed and tested, but systems procedures include several important aspects of implementation. One is feedback. This effort continues throughout the operation of the system in order to determine:

1. The continuing effectiveness of the system or the need for changes

2. The continuing relevance of the system in terms of its objectives

3. The need for the creation of new systems as a result of changing objectives, new developments, or new criteria for selecting alternatives.

Feedback systems impose several requirements on the design and execution of a system. An effective feedback system must be designed and implemented at the beginning of the process. Briefly, this entails the collection of information about inputs and environment; the formulation of statements of goals and purposes; and, at critical points throughout the operation of the system and designated concluding points, the collection of output information for comparison with the original data. In this way, the effectiveness and efficiency of the system can be measured. Appropriate adjustments can be made in the system's operation based on this information or in conformance with changing goals or standards.

Traditional teacher education programs have been especially weak in this kind of feedback system. Lacking a clear-cut statement of goals related to the development of teaching competencies, programs have generally produced young teachers who are liberally educated and who have been exposed to some aspects of teaching—usually from a distance. The relation of these training experiences to the real world of teaching remains unclear, but adjustments are difficult because there is no feedback system—in this case, data from the teacher and the school district to the institution preparing the teachers, in a form encouraging program adjustment—that permits analysis and control of the system.

Another important aspect of implementation is the ability of the institutions to accept new systems. Some universities and colleges of education are unable to make the necessary adjustments; others, seeing the need for change, have undertaken projects to improve their teacher education programs. Federally funded programs have frequently provided opportunities for experimentation and development that could not be financed otherwise. Cooperative planning by colleges and state and local agencies, based on mutual goals and shared responsibilities, is preparing the way for incorporation of new and effective approaches to teacher education.

The nature of the planning and design process frequently determines the kinds of problems encountered during implementation. Most system analysis and design efforts fail to be useful because they do not explain the whole system; or, if they purposely describe only part of a system, they cannot be related to the rest of it. Educational planning has been particularly guilty in this respect. School operating units are sometimes totally separated from the designers and producers of materials, and both remain apart from the colleges and universities producing the teachers. Small wonder then that many new teachers are unprepared to cope with the realities of the classroom.

A complete systems design for teacher education should trace the process from the student's entry through his initial years of teaching. In other words, it should include both preservice and inservice components in a common structure. The design should also describe the linkages between the college of education or teacher education program, now defined as a subsystem, and other parts of the education system; trace the flow of information and resources among these subsystems; and specify the areas of independent and cooperative action.

Constraints on Systems Planning in General

The design of any system is limited by many factors, some of them negotiable, but many of them beyond the control of the systems designer. In systems terminology, these limits are known as constraints. Deciding which constraints will affect a systems operation is an important aspect of the design process. In a sense, systems designers are fortunate; they can design ideal systems without considering the day-to-day real-world operations that can clog even the best designs. This approach, however, has frequently permitted the creation of beautifully engineered systems that are totally incompatible with their environments. On the other hand, unless designers consider carefully just how real some assumed barriers are, their field of vision will be limited, and the system will fail to cope with the true problems. In planning programs for teacher education, the following general constraints are significant:

Time
A teacher must be educated in four years of college, or five

years if the masters program is included. It is easy to conceive programs taking less time, either through reevaluation of educational requirements or through increased efficiency in the training processes. Basing programs on goal achievement rather than on time boundaries would permit a more reasonable apportionment of time among required areas of study, experience, and on-the-job practice. Time has been the traditional value measurement in education, but as more agencies accept competency measurement instead of course credit, time restrictions will become less significant for program planning.

Data

We have not yet developed adequate knowledge for good program design, particularly in the area of the relationship between a teacher's behavior and a student's learning. The Elementary Teacher Education Models recognize these limits and have suggested new and significant areas of research and development. They have also presented feedback designs of one form or another in which information from practice is a major source of data for program adjustment and redesign.

The Scope of the System

The broader the initial conception of the system, the stronger will be the design of any subuniverse. For example, a major weakness of teaching has been the classroom teacher's inability—due to press of time and responsibilities—to get beyond the four walls of the classroom and interact with other colleagues. This condition contributes to a narrowing concept of education and an inability to view the educational process as continuous. Thus, the relationship between the first and sixth grades is often blurred, subjects are repeated, and students are confined to a limited curriculum.

A significant change in recent educational planning has been a recognition of the broad complex of institutions and organizations affecting the design and operation of the system. Program planners have become increasingly concerned with analysis of the roles of government agencies (especially at the federal level), education industries, and education oriented foundations. Such developments as educational vouchers, behavior modification, and day care "packaging" may bring industrial and research organizations into direct competition with the schools. New design activities must acknowledge these changes and the principles underlying them. They mark the development of a new "energy level" for education and, perhaps, an effective means for challenging persistent educational problems.

Communications

The relationships between teacher education programs and the other parts of the university are sometimes counterproductive because neither has sufficient or accurate information about the other. The designers of several elementary teacher education projects have found that while they were trying to develop individualized and competency based course work, their students still had to meet university course and credit requirements in order to graduate. Some school systems have developed operational linkages with many universities, industries, educational organizations, and other groups. This process of increasing communications channels extends the concept of the system and the program of education beyond their traditional limits.

System Integration

It is possible to design a beautiful system, which is consonant with our view of reality, but which fails to operate simply because it does not conform to the real world of other system designs. If an educational system produces teachers who are unable to function in harmony with teachers trained in other systems, communication will be limited and friction will result. The process of obviating this difficulty is called system integration. It requires that the designers of a system—regardless of how complete the system is—be concerned with its ability to mesh with other systems. An educational program that does not produce the kind of labor force required in the future will not serve the needs of the economic system; similarly, a school system that cannot educate a large percentage of its students cannot claim absolute control over the process of education.

This concept does not require that the designers of innovative programs sacrifice some of their more innovative ideas; they simply must develop an awareness of integration problems. Effective change and implementation procedures can usually be developed, unless the new program represents a radical departure from the values of the former one. Systems designers must carefully weigh their position and develop linkages for integrating program changes.

Facilities

We are rarely able to design a program, and then build a suitable building. Usually the program is constrained by the preexisting building. New techniques such as modular walls, inside-outside rooms, and heat, light, and sound controls (for example, the multimedia rooms with student response systems) offer fewer constraints on program planning than do the facilities in older buildings, but they are still constraints. The location of activities can play an important part in the nature and quality of an experience. Watching pupils in a classroom—and actually taking part in their activities—can result in perceptions quite different from those achieved by observing a movie in a college lecture hall. Since it is particularly difficult to change extant facilities, careful planning should precede their development, but careful planning can also obviate many of the apparent constraints of present facilities.

Resources

To a systems analyst, there are many types of resources. The most obvious one, of course, is money. Others include teacher time, student time, equipment, space, expertise, information, and other institutions. The list of potential resources can be quite long, but frequently a system fails to incorporate the broad number of resources available to it. Consideration of these resources may suggest alternative systems that conserve the critical resource: the one most difficult to replace. In education we have generally assumed that the student's time was the least valuable resource. In fact, to the student at least, his time is a critical resource, and we should plan programs to make effective use of it.

Constraints on Teacher Education Programs

The above constraints apply to the design of any program and every planner, but in the field of teacher education there are in addition several specific constraints. Some of these define the limits of potential programs, because they can be modified only within fixed limits. Indeed, changing them requires changing our perceptions of teachers in rather radical ways. This may be a necessary concomitant to the improvement of teacher education, but it is a slow process.

Certification Requirements

Each state sets minimum standards for the certification of professional persons. Historically, for teachers these requirements have been based solely on the completion of one or two college degrees and some special courses in education. A recent trend, however, has been for the state to authorize colleges to certify as a teacher any person who completes its state approved program of preparation. The problem is that certification is still based on completion of courses and hours of credit. The need is for measures of teaching proficiencies and statements of entry level competencies based on teacher functions and roles. Certification can then be based on these standards rather than on the present formal criteria. The net result of this change will be to focus on output—the quality of the teacher—rather than on process—the awarding of degrees. This development will further permit exploring alternative preparations programs, such as beginning as a teacher aide and advancing to full status by means of experience and inservice training, rather than by means of a college degree.

Local and State Personnel Policies

Personnel policies are established to govern the behavior of individuals within complex organizations. Usually large institutions require some form of structure to promote their purposes, but personnel policies often reject individuals who might make a positive contribution. For instance, how many persons choose not to teach because of policies against beards, alternate life-styles, or unconventional costumes? The schools are becoming more tolerant of, or at least sensitive to, individual differences, but these policies still exert a strong pressure on the acculturation aspects of teacher education programs. These programs too often emphasize "adjusting to the realities of teaching" rather than "developing the person as a teacher."

Individual School Administrators

The school administrator usually has almost complete control over his school and athletic field. Thus, his style of leadership determines both the tone of the school and its educational quality, since he usually selects teachers with whom he can get along. While this management technique appears reasonable, it can prevent diversity and limit the kinds of experiences available to students. It can also mean that some schools will not accept teachers produced by innovative programs. A systems approach to this problem would be to assure that the administrators are as carefully selected and trained—in terms of the same goal oriented procedures—as teachers.

The Profession

The teaching profession, often conservative and inbred, tends to fear radical departures from present practices. Professionally acceptable teacher activism most notably concerns itself with pay and prestige rather than with problems of change and education. In this situation, a new breed of teacher—militant, liberal, and action oriented—is often defeated by conservative colleagues and unresponsive school systems and communities. Nevertheless, it is clear that little progress could have been made in American education without an organized profession of teachers.

It is also clear that whatever its prevailing philosophy is, the profession has the power, through its several agencies and organizations, to influence, direct, and censure many practices in teacher education. In some respects, a profession is an inhibitor of change. Those who are "in" will try to keep others out until the "outs" come to look like the "ins." This is as much an unconscious effect of professionalism as a direct threat to programs of preparation, but the accepted philosophy of the professional groups interacting with a teacher preparation program will in large part affect that program's ability to achieve its goals. (A possible alternative would be for the profession to accept responsibility for training, thus removing it from the college. The entire educational system in this case might be radically different. The problem appears to be one of adjusting bureaucratic acculturation or system maintenance needs to the flexibility required by new programs and approaches to the teaching roles.)

Teacher Candidates

Teacher education programs must be responsive to the persons who apply for admittance. During the past two decades numerous authors have pointed out that the least able university student enters the field of education, and quality programs consequently must be "watered down." Other writers have suggested with equal force that good programs will attract strong candidates. There is virtue in both positions. Still other studies indicate that even graduates of strong programs leave teaching after three to five years unless they have adapted to conform to the existing limitations of the school. At best the very conditions of teaching seem to limit the effectiveness of strong college programs. Competency based programs, however, set realistic standards for admittance and graduation. Such planning should have a strong influence on the selection of teacher candidates.

Information and Systems

Systems analysis evolved as an information oriented, decision-making process. In this respect systems designs are based on the requirements of getting and organizing information. Four kinds of information are usually specified: (1) input, (2) output, (3) process, and (4) environment. To express this concept in basic terms, we want to know:

1. What was the student like when he entered the program? What do we want him to be like at the end of the program, i.e., what are the goals of the program?

2. What was the student like at the end of the program, i.e., what new knowledge and skills did he have? Did the program achieve its goals, i.e., did the student acquire the knowledge and skills we wanted him to?

3. How did the program achieve its goals? Assuming it was effective, did it operate efficiently as designed?

All these questions in the last analysis are "situation specific," that is, they operate within a specific environment. Therefore we also want to know:

4. Was the process an acceptable system within the operating environment? Did it change the environment? Did the environment change the system? What adjustments were required because of constraints on the program?

A feedback system is explicitly developed as part of a systems design. Changes in the system may be made because of information received through operating the system or because of changes in the environment. Similarly, the environment provides information on needs, and this information affects the priorities assigned to various processes. For example, if it is important to produce teachers strong in arithmetic and science skills, the program can be adjusted accordingly. The particular information requirements of a teacher education model will vary according to the design of the system, its definition of the teacher, and its relationship to the environment; therefore, it is difficult to do more than suggest the importance of designing a system based on information rather than on past experiences, guesswork, or luck. In this respect systems analysis provides a realistic framework for applying the results of research and other feedback activities to the improvement of the teacher education process.

System Objectives in Teacher Education

The preceding discussion has provided a process for determining the objectives of a teacher education program and has indicated some of the difficulties in achieving adequate statements of objectives. Two guidelines are useful in formulating these statements:

1. State alternative series of objectives based on the profiles of individual students. Since any program will service a variety of students, objectives should be stated that are compatible with their various abilities. Thus, each student's program will be unique, but each program will contribute to achieving the general goals and objectives of teacher education. In a sense, each student could be thought of as a subsystem, representing a unique input and output and presenting a unique confrontation of process and environment. In this respect it is possible to establish the basis for individualized programs of instruction.

2. Keep the process of explicating objectives flexible and responsive to changing patterns of teaching and learning. This consideration is really a reminder that systems procedures are constantly reiterative processes. One does not state objectives and then pass on to the next steps in the process. Both changes in the environment and measurements from the operation of the process will affect the statement and ordering of objectives. It appears highly desirable to assess the value of the objectives and the ability of the process to meet them. Otherwise, even a carefully designed program will atrophy.

A second form of goal setting focuses on the operation of the system. These goals concentrate first on the processes the system will use to affect groups of students and then on the effective management of the system. Programming, Planning, and Budgeting Systems (PPBS) and other cost-effectiveness techniques are designed to help assess the operation of systems in relation to previously stated goals. The establishment of goals for the entire system is important, because it permits the efficient and effective selection of alternatives. For educational planning, however, concentration on the system may preclude an adequate view of the final product, the student.

The system procedures techniques, developed for the design and delivery of hardware systems and their required support systems, tend to concentrate on aspects other than the individual. They are appropriate to the design of such technological systems as educational television, mobile facilities, or computer systems, but once these systems are designed, they must be seen simply as means for the achievement of goals relating to the individual. This consideration suggests that a dynamic interaction should be maintained between these two design levels to ensure that the system fits its essential purposes.

The question of an appropriate statement of objectives within the framework of systems procedures has received considerable attention, especially since these techniques have begun to move into the social sphere. There is no doubt that the effectiveness of deliberate systems design and analysis is increased by the degree to which goals can be objectified and objectives made explicit. Some writers have gone so far as to suggest that systems analysis represents a viable approach only in situations where the goals permit quantifiable measurement, but this position remains extreme.

Even if the whole of teacher education cannot be explicated and quantified, because the whole of teaching as an art somehow defies analysis, the systematic planning of many experiences can still be undertaken. The physical properties of color have been explicated and can be known by every budding artist. Although this knowledge will not guarantee a Picasso, it is highly unlikely that Picasso could paint without such basic information. In exactly the same sense, the teacher will operate as an individual person with his pupils, but he can be trained in many of the skills and techniques that will facilitate his performance.

The Total Design Process

The effective application of systems procedures in education requires viewing the total design process as composed of three interrelated but distinct aspects: the task of systems design, the analysis of the system environment, and the change or implementation process. Figure 2 provides a graphic representation of these elements and the necessary intercommunication among them.

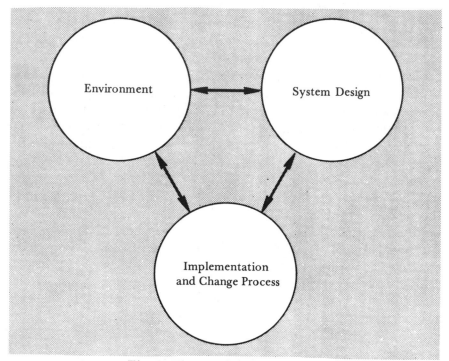

Fig. 2. The total design process

The system design process has yielded highly sophisticated engineering systems, but this process has not been functionally interrelated to either the system environment or the change and implementation process. The systems approach begins with a premise that the educational enterprise achieves its apparent objectives primarily through people, rather than through machines. Furthermore, the systems approach of industry must be modified if it is to serve school enterprises properly, since industrial organizations generally use rigid barometers to indicate degree of success and failures—such as profit or loss statements, measurement of tangible products, and quality assurance standards—while school systems have generally operated in the absence of such definable criteria. A basic belief in the entire concept of applying systems procedures to the educational environment is that if the systems concept is to be helpful to educators, it is important to recognize that schools exist primarily to facilitate goals related to student learning.

If education is regarded as a system, it follows that problems neither exist nor can be solved in isolation from the total system. The system's environment must also be considered since it is the primary location of both system constraints and system resources. The environment includes both explicit and implicit political, economic, and social forces that impinge on the system. It causes system problems, and it can also provide problem solutions. For instance, suppose there were a program of training for all expectant mothers, emphasizing child growth and development. Such an alternative might produce greater results than similar expenditures for additional preschools, nursery-level educational television, or for some other scheme. This essentially educational program, however, while affecting the K-12 input and thus the educational system, would require changes in areas beyond the limits of the ordinary school system, as well as adaptive changes within it.

The literature on change and implementation appears to be growing by leaps and bounds both within and outside the field of education, and development models have improved the evaluation effort. Feedback relating input and output is beginning to yield some effective observations about educational programs. It may be too soon to place strong faith in analyses of critical factors and predictions based on them, but they have certainly become useful and important guides to judgment.

The three areas of system design, system environment, and the change process, have not received sufficient attention as integral parts of a single process for discovering and implementing educational improvements. As a result there is little compatible information on which to develop the potential effects of changes in one aspect of the total process or in the whole process. For instance, deciding whether to change the system or redefine the environments can seldom be adequately handled by present experimental techniques, both because essential factors are not always known and because alternative environments in education are seldom considered.

Consequences

The application of systems procedures to the planning, design, and operation of educational processes remains controversial. Nevertheless, the application of a comprehensive, step-by-step, total planning process to education appears to offer the following advantages:

1. A comprehensive, long-range view of large-scale problems within a productive framework for understanding the processes and functions inherent within the system

2. A basis for developing goal oriented programs that are sensitive to the environment and changing context of education

3. A method for the effective organization of parts into meaningful problem oriented frameworks

4. An analysis of alternative allocations of resources based on the relation of resources to goal achievement within the process of educational change

5. A context for understanding the constraints imposed on the institutional structure of education

6. A group of planning techniques that make possible the large-scale, long-range planning of integrated educational programs

7. An interdisciplinary, problem oriented approach to research and development based on the organization of information for the solution of problems

On the other hand, systems procedures are no mystical, scientific cure-all for the complex problems implied by changes in educational technology, teacher roles, learning goals, or changing patterns of educational resources. Some important limits include:

1. Systems procedures cannot show ways to operate below certain necessary minimums.

2. They cannot remove the constraints imposed by institutional force, but they may suggest ways to work around them.

3. Systems analysis cannot compensate for a lack of clear-cut purpose or for a confused operational philosophy.

4. Systems analysis cannot provide simplistic procedures for arriving at incontestable conclusions.

5. There can be no guarantee that procedures developed in one discipline will be automatically transferable to another field.

6. Systems analysis cannot replace judgments or the necessity for decision making.

Teacher education programs have benefited from the use of analysis procedures as applied by each of the ten Elementary Teacher Education Models. These projects have developed strong bases for the future direction of educational planning, design, and operation. These techniques will require continued modification and improvement, but the direction toward systematic, integrated, long-range educational planning has been clearly established.

References

Adams, Don, ed. *Educational Planning.* Syracuse, New York: Center for Development Education, Syracuse University Press, 1964.

American Association of School Administrators. *Administrative Technology.* Edited by Stephen J. Knezevich. Washington, D.C.: National Education Association, 1969.

Banghart, Frank W. *Educational Systems Analysis.* New York: Macmillan, 1969.

Boguslaw, Robert. *The New Utopians: A Study of Systems Design and Social Change.* Englewood Cliffs, N.J.: Prentice-Hall, 1965.

Coombs, Philip H. *The World Educational Crisis: A Systems Analysis.* New York: Oxford University Press, 1968.

Hartley, Harry J. *Educational Planning-Programming-Budgeting: A Systems Approach.* Englewood Cliffs, N.J.: Prentice-Hall, 1969.

LeBaron, Walt. *Elementary Teacher Education Models Analyzed in Relation to National Accreditation Standards.* Washington, D.C.: American Association of Colleges for Teacher Education, July 1970.

——. "Technological Forces and the Teacher's Changing Role." *Journal of Teacher Education* 20 (Winter 1969): 451–464.

Morphet, Edgar L. & Jesser, David L., eds. *Planning for Effective Utilization of Technology in Education.* Denver, Colo.: Designing Education for the Future, 1968.

O'Toole, John F. *Systems Analysis and Decision-Making in Education.* Santa Monica, Calif.: Systems Development Corp., 1965.

Sackman, Harold. *Computers, Systems Science, and Evolving Society: The Challenge of Man-Machine Digital Systems.* New York: John Wiley & Sons, 1967.

Skinner, B. F. *The Technology of Teaching.* New York: Appleton-Century-Crofts, 1968.

Smith, Robert G., Jr. *The Design of Instruction Systems.* Alexandria, Va.: Human Resources Research Organization (HumRRO), George Washington University, 1966.

Systems Analysis for Educational Planning: An Annotated Bibliography. Paris: Organization for Economic Cooperation & Development, 1969.

3

The Personalization of Teacher Education Programs

H. Del Schalock

Jesse Garrison

For teacher education to be relevant and humanistic in its orientation, it must be personalized. To be personalized, it requires both face-to-face personal contacts and a variety of strategies that individualize the instruction-learning process.[1]

Position

The personalization of teacher education programs requires careful attention to four aspects of curriculum planning and implementation: (1) the need to consider ways and means of bringing the learner into face-to-face contact with instructors and peers throughout the instruction-learning process; (2) the need to meet individual differences throughout the process; (3) the need to provide the learner with opportunities to participate in the design of his personal instruction-learning plan; and (4) the need to involve the learner significantly in the design and development of the larger program of which his personal plan is a part.

Rationale

The term *personalization* conveys meanings beyond those implied by the term *individualization*. The latter refers generally to providing students with opportunities for independent learning. Individualization of instruction ranges from differentiating one learner from the next only by the rate at which a particular sequence of activities is undertaken to differentiating by providing optional sequences, instructional modes, or entry-exit points within each learning sequence. Such instruction, though individualized, does not assure a humanistic learning environment. In fact, it is quite possible to individualize in a manner that contributes significantly to the dehumanization of instruction. Personalization avoids this pitfall by both individualizing instruction and requiring instructors and others to help a learner select what he wants to learn and the ways of learning it.

In a program committed to personalization, individualization of the program provides both a wide range of learning experiences (instructional materials) for any given learning outcome, and a wide range of learning outcomes; thus, a learner may choose both the ends and the means that suit him best. Each learning experience must be provided at the time deemed critical by the learner. The individualization of instruction cannot take place in a meager environment. A variety of instructional sequences must exist to offer learners choices in meeting personal learning needs.

Personalized learning recognizes the learner as an equal in setting the objectives in a learning program, and allows the learner to decide his use of these objectives. The personalization of a teacher education program must provide for students' individual characteristics and commitments. The central concern of the personalized program is to allow and encourage an infinite variety of human potential. It acknowledges the tension between the individual and "the system"; between the past and the future; between what is and what ought to be.

Personalization requires that students have a continuing impact on the design, development, and operational implementation of the program in which they are participating. Alienation of students and irrelevance of education stem partially from the fact that students often do not help determine the nature of their learning experiences. Student participation in program planning at a variety of levels would make the program reflect basic student expectations and thus help students recognize the program as partly theirs.

Conditions Necessary for Implementation

Specific Person-to-Person Experiences

The personalized teacher education program is envisioned as including heavy use of independent study. Such study occurs as students individually pursue a given objective; in doing so they can draw on various resources, including literature, visual presentations, computer assisted instruction, and various combinations of these modes. These learning experiences must be supplemented by formal and informal person-to-person experiences. Formal personal experiences are designed into learning sequences, and instructional staff should be prepared to facilitate students' study, at appropriate times and in appropriate ways within these sequences. Envisioned are seminars, conferences with instructional staff, conferences for purposes of assessing progress, and a variety of instances in which pairs or groups of students work together to solve a given problem presented in simulated format or in other modes. Informal person-to-person experience requires that learning spaces be designed to bring students together naturally as they participate in the learning environment. This informality extends to the easy availability of faculty who can create small spur-of-the-moment seminars among interested students seeking clarification of their own ideas.

If personalization of instruction is to succeed, we must significantly change our concepts of faculty roles, faculty-student relationships, and institutional expectations. A new blending of technology and humanistic values and of independent study and group exploration of ideas is imperative. There is no greater educational challenge in sight for the seventies, none will come under closer scrutiny, and none is more essential to the success of the kind of teacher education program sought by those who would personalize teacher education.

Variety of Instructional Options

Many educators think programs in schools today are individualized because they allow differences in the rates at which learners move through a set of instructional experiences. Rate has been a popular focus for individualization, not because rate differences are of supreme importance, but because they are the most easily identified variable. Many variables in learning have not yet been identified. A few have been identified, and we need to focus attention and planning efforts on those. For example, we know that learning styles vary. We know that, while some learners benefit most from direct instruction, others learn best through inductive processes. We know that reading is effective for some but others find other media more effective. Although we know learners vary in these and other dimensions, we have too little evidence to identify which learners will benefit from which instructional modes. Current research in aptitude/treatment interaction will benefit future plans to personalize education. Further, as personalized programs become operational and include a greater variety of instructional modes, more can be learned about aptitude variables and their interaction with instructional treatments.

Student Participation in Design of Their Own Programs

Some educational research has indicated that more learning occurs when learners are able to choose their learning or instructional mode than when they are directed to it. This implies that within the overall teacher education program, each student should be able to negotiate a personally relevant program.

Operationally this will probably involve negotiation within three categories of competencies: (1) those required of all students; (2) those required of a student who chooses to prepare for teaching in a field requiring specialization, such as preschool or special education; and (3) those requested by a student. This means the content of each student's program will vary by interest, specialization, background of knowledge and skill, and personal learning style. Negotiation means negotiation: students and the representatives of the program must arrive at a program of work that is mutually satisfying, given the information and range of choices available.

Three requirements must be met if a personalized program is to succeed:

1. A large store of information on interests, objectives, and performance history must be available to both students and faculty so that informed decisions on programs can be made.

2. The whole program must be flexible enough to permit fairly free movement among learning experiences within various phases of the program and some movement across phases.

3. Faculty must have the sensitivities and capabilities that permit meaningful negotiation. It is hoped that the first can be accomplished by a computer based information management system and the other two by careful faculty selection and effective inservice education.

If personalization of instruction is to be extended to its logical end, students have two additional negotiations to make after they have negotiated the competencies they are to demonstrate:

1. The settings within which they will demonstrate these competencies. This will involve specifying the outcome a student is attempting to realize; the pupils, parents, or peers to be involved in the situation; and the physical characteristics of the setting.

2. The behaviors or products of behavior that can be considered evidence of competence.

Once this level of detail has been specified and accepted, the tasks of both the prospective teacher and the person responsible for assessing his performance become manageable and relatively clear.

The same general strategy can be followed in mastering the knowledge and sensitivities thought prerequisite to demonstrating competence.

Finally, in order to ensure maximum relevance to both the ends being pursued by a student and the means to those ends, all instructional programs need an element that impels the prospective teacher to assess the consistency of his goals, his commitment to them, and their influence on his evolving teaching style. One procedure for this is a "corrective decision loop" attached to all instructional experiences. The corrective decision loop operates when it appears the goal being purused is invalid or when the student fails to perform at criterion level. In either case, the student is channeled into the corrective decision loop where he can explore through conference the relevance of the ends he is pursuing or the means he is using. Every instructional experience needs such a procedure.

Student Participation in Design
and Development of Overall Program

In the decades ahead educational programs will be increasingly formed by a more widely based power group. Neither administrators, university personnel, public school teachers, students, nor any other single group will decide the nature of instructional programs in the future. Power will reside in committees: conglomerates of these various groups and institutional representatives. Increasingly, these groups will include students. The contributions of these students will help keep programs congruent with their interests and needs.

In the past year or so, campus committees have often included token student representation, but their presence alone is not enough. Students must genuinely participate in designing programs in teacher education.

Mechanism for Personalization

Three vehicles are needed to facilitate wise and personally valid choice: (1) sponsorship, (2) clinical supervision, and (3) negotiation. As used here, *sponsorship* means a continuing relationship between a faculty member and a student throughout the student's stay in the program. The aim of the sponsor-student relationship is to permit two people to see each other as individuals—with needs, pressures, and limits—so that reasonable negotiation can occur between them. To make this contact more than superficial a sponsor will be responsible for no more than fifteen or twenty students.

The *clinical supervisor* is a school based person who assumes primary responsibility for the student's instruction, assessment, and welfare while he is within the school setting. As such, the clinical supervisor works closely with the sponsor throughout the program and assumes many of the sponsor's functions when the student is in the field. A clinical supervisor, too, will be responsible for only a small number of students.

Within the context of a personalized program, *negotiation* is to be taken literally, i.e., the parties involved hold positions open to change. A student will interact with his sponsor and his clinical supervisor to negotiate his total program.

The sponsor-student relationship begins as soon as the student declares an interest in the teacher education program; the sponsor-student-clinical supervisor relationship begins as soon as a student enters the clinical studies phase of the program. The rationale underlying the sponsorship and negotiation strategy is straightforward: responsibility for program and professional standards must be ensured, but not at the price of denying the individuality of students in the program. One way of accommodating both is to provide a mechanism for genuine negotiation between individuals representing both concerns. Whenever genuine and fruitful negotiations cannot occur, sponsorship must be changed. The request for change may come from either student or sponsor.

As in any negotiation procedure, provision must be made for arbitration when successful negotiation cannot be carried out. It is proposed that this be provided by an arbitration board consisting of a student, a college faculty member, and a staff member from the public schools. Given a functional student-sponsor relationship and ground rules requiring them to understand that the outcome of any given negotiation is to be acceptable to both parties, we anticipate little need for arbitration.

Student and Staff Attitudes

We cannot discuss personalization without dealing with the problem of people's differing perceptions. Two people viewing academic material, a learning situation, or an instance of behavior are going to view it differently. If they are to be capable of working together, however, their perceptions cannot be too divergent. This is especially critical in a personalized program where individual differences are emphasized and movement depends on negotiation. Considerable care must be taken, therefore, that perceptions of students and sponsors are compatible enough to support the planning-negotiation-assessing process.

Fortunately, close contact among sponsor, clinical supervisor, and student from the beginning of a personalized program should permit the necessary sharing of perceptions. It is hoped each will come to understand the others' perception of the meaning and significance of events. From such a relationship trust, respect, and sensitivity can grow; a personalized program cannot operate without these qualities.

One final consideration: a basic assumption underlying the personalization of a teacher education program is that those engaging in it have enough understanding of their own goals, commitments, preferences, and capabilities to make wise decisions. In other words, there must be sufficient self-understanding by both students and faculty for useful personalization to exist. Since self-understanding is an illusive quality and seems to be in short supply, an essential element of a personalized teacher education program is a set of learning experiences to abet self-understanding. These must be encountered early and continuously, since the demands on staff and students in a competency based program vary as progress is made.

Assessment Consistent with Philosophy of Personalization

Given the three classes of criteria in a competency based program—knowledge, skills, products—and the need to personalize criteria at each level, assessment must be modified considerably from what it is in most programs. Instead of being norm referenced, it must become criteria referenced; and instead of measuring individual performance relative to group performance independent of context, it must measure each person's performance by standards appropriate to that person in a specific context. Some of the consequences of such a shift in focus will be illustrated in the following paragraphs as they pertain to the assessment of product outcomes: that is, the ability of prospective teachers to precipitate specific outcomes in pupils or to perform tasks such as curriculum development and evaluation. Similar suggestions apply, however, to the assessment of skills and, to some extent, to the assessment of knowledge.

1. When competence is to be assessed in terms of the products deriving from a teacher's behavior, evidence must be obtained that a pupil or set of pupils can read or are more considerate of the feelings of others; or curriculum or materials development efforts have in fact been productive; or parents do understand a school's policy on reporting pupil performance.

2. Seeking the products of a teacher's behavior to assess competency means that competency is always situation specific. In other words, competency in instruction must always be thought of as the ability to cause a specific outcome in a specific child or set of children who have specific characteristics and who are in a specific setting. For example, competency might be getting a six-year-old child in a class of ten, who is bright but visually handicapped, to distinguish the letters of the alphabet; or getting a thirteen-year-old boy of average ability in a class of thirty, with little exposure to cultures other than his own isolated mountain community, to value other cultures.

3. Since it is situation specific, competency must always be

demonstrated in a real-life setting. Real pupils working toward real objectives must be available if students are to demonstrate competency as instructors. Real parents or real curriculum development projects must be available if they are to demonstrate instructional support competencies.

4. Before students attempt to demonstrate competency in ongoing educational settings, colleges, schools, and state departments of education should establish procedures to determine in advance whether a prospective teacher can perform at least adequately in a real-life setting. For example, a teacher might be required to demonstrate competence under laboratory or simplified conditions before assuming supervised responsibility for children's learning in a school. The assumption underlying such a requirement is twofold: laboratory or simulated conditions permit the demonstration of competence under circumstances where (1) the complexity of the teaching-learning situation is controlled, and (2) the possibility of negative consequences for children is reduced. Once a prospective teacher has demonstrated competence under simplified conditions, we may assume he can enter actual classroom situations, with supervision, and perform well.

5. To ensure that a prospective teacher is broadly competent, he may be required to demonstrate each competence in a variety of settings. Since the number of possible settings is endless, this strategy of assessment requires situations that appropriately sample classes of educational settings. As indicated earlier, a basic assumption of personalized education is that each prospective teacher will negotiate the specific situations in which to demonstrate his competency and that these situations will reflect the types of situations in which he will actually teach.

Consequences

Teachers Can Demonstrate Specific Competency

The opportunity to negotiate the competencies to be developed, the contexts within which to demonstrate them, and the criteria by which to be judged—especially since these are negotiated from self-understanding—provides an unfettered chance for teaching students to identify and engage in a program uniquely suited to them as individuals. Since they are responsible for the definition-negotiation of their own programs and are held accountable for demonstrating the competencies they have negotiated, teachers emerging from the program should understand clearly what they want to do, and what they can do. If this is so, a data dependent, personalized program should reduce complaints of irrelevance and superficiality within teacher education. This clarity will help resolve the old conflict between public accountability and humanism.

Teachers with Different "Styles" Can Produce Predictable Outcomes

Not only do prospective teachers learn different things, in accordance with their interests, backgrounds, and skills, but they also learn things in different ways. To get outcome A, for example, one teacher may use behaviors X, Y, and Z; another teacher may use behaviors Z, W, and M—yet each teacher may successfully reach the desired outcome. A personalized teacher education program admits these differences and nurtures them. There is a profound respect for the complexity of matching strategies and content to various kinds of learners in different settings to bring about a given outcome. There is an equally profound respect for the variety of ways teachers can put these factors together at any one time.

Teachers Can Provide Personalized and Data Dependent Instruction

There is reason to believe that when prospective teachers engage in education that is data dependent and personalized, thus becoming independent, self-directing learners themselves, they can and will create a similar learning environment for the children they teach.

Footnotes

1. A number of persons have asked how the concept of personalization outlined in this chapter differs from the concept used by Robert Peck and his colleagues in the Center for Research and Development in Teacher Education at the University of Texas. It differs, as we see it, in terms of the *focus* of the personalization experience. In the present chapter, the personalization of teacher education refers to the process by which the learning environments of students in teacher education are personalized. As Peck and his associates use the term, the personalization of teacher education refers to the preparation of prospective teachers in such a way that they will be able to personalize the learning environ-

ments of pupils. For a recent review of the work of Peck and his associates in this regard, see R. F. Peck, "Promoting Self-Disciplined Learning: A Researchable Revolution," in *Research in Teacher Education,* B. O. Smith, ed. (Englewood Cliffs, N. J.: Prentice-Hall, 1971), pp. 82–98.

4

Competency Based Teacher Preparation

Norman R. Dodl

H. Del Schalock

Position

We are committed to the use of competency based criteria for teacher preparation and certification. Students and, ultimately, teachers must be held accountable for the realization of these criteria. Their realization must be based on acquired knowledge, demonstrated performance, and predictable products.

In the decades ahead, teachers will be held increasingly accountable for their behavior. The movement toward behavioral accountability has arisen partly from the conviction that desired educational outcomes can be specified and measured with reasonable precision, and partly from the increase in parent-community concern and involvement in the direction and operation of local public education. The teaching profession, while working steadily toward public recognition of its professional status, has found that it must deal realistically with the issue of accountability.

The increased emphasis on accountability has been paralleled by the increased use of systems approaches in designing teacher education programs. Although it is difficult to identify precisely the factors that explain this movement, it is clear that increased costs of funding quality educational experiences require improved effectiveness and efficiency in teacher education.

In the next decade or two the concepts of accountability and systems design will produce teacher preparation programs that include the systematic specification of learning goals, teaching behaviors that can best effect those goals, and attitudes and feelings that contribute to a healthy climate for learning. Professional licensure to teach will be based on demonstrated competencies defined in terms of knowledge, teacher behavior, and specified pupil outcomes.

Rationale

Competency based teacher preparation derives from instructional activities designed and implemented to produce teachers who possess designated competencies for entry into the teaching profession. Traditionally, the competencies for entering the teaching profession have been defined ambiguously if at all. State departments of education offer the most readily available indicators of traditional expectancies in their requirements for teaching certificates. Almost without exception, these are stated in terms of required courses and time served in student teaching or internships. Demonstrations of competency will supersede evidence of courses passed and time spent in student teaching as certification requirements.

The lack of clearly defined outcomes hampers traditional teacher education processes. Even when sufficient time for teaching practice is provided, this lack of specific performance criteria makes it impossible to measure either the effects of training on performance or the student's readiness to enter the teaching profession. Competency based teacher preparation is designed to overcome this handicap.

As the teaching profession moves toward accountability, the point of view represented by a competency based approach assumes the following:

1. Rigorous criteria for knowing, as well as systematic specification of what is to be known (knowledge), must be a part of teacher education.

2. Knowing and the ability to apply what is known (performance) are two different matters.

3. The ability to attain specified objectives with learners (product) represents still another kind of competency that will be required of teacher candidates.

4. The criteria for assessing what a prospective teacher can do

(performance) should be as rigorous, as systematically derived, and as explicitly stated as the criteria for assessing either what he knows (knowledge) or what he can achieve in learners (product).

5. Assessments of knowledge, performance, and product must be described and made systematically.

6. Only when a prospective teacher has the appropriate knowledge, can perform in a stipulated manner, and can produce anticipated results with learners, will he meet competency based requirements.

The assessment criteria for a competency based teacher preparation program are illustrated in figure 1.

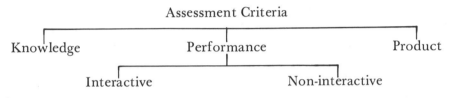

Fig. 1. Assessment criteria for a competency based
teacher preparation program

Traditional teacher preparation programs were concerned primarily with knowledge criteria for the assessment of objectives. Recently, however, the programs have begun to shift toward assessment procedures that emphasize performance criteria, and it can be expected that performance criteria will constitute a major force for innovation in education during the next decade. Both interactive and noninteractive behaviors are types of teacher performances that must form part of the basis of teaching competence. For instance, if teachers must use probing questions effectively to assist pupils to extend and clarify concepts, a prospective teacher must demonstrate that he can effectively use such questions with pupils. Such teacher behavior will be evaluated both on its quality and on the frequency of its occurrence. An example of noninteractive teacher behavior is the ability to select, using a stated set of criteria, instructional materials that suit each learner's abilities and objectives. If the selection criteria are explicit, the assessment of this instructionally related but noninteractive behavior can be reasonably precise.

We have defined competency as the realization of publicly specified criteria for classes of learning outcomes found to be appropriate to teacher preparation, i.e., knowledge, skills (performance), and products. With regard to this mix, we suggest that, in spite of the methodological problems encountered thus far in teacher effectiveness research,[1] the ability to bring about specified learning outcomes in pupils will be included as one of the criteria on which to assess teacher competence. The mix of these classes of learning outcomes will depend on a variety of factors and will differ substantially from program to program.

Using product based criteria to assess teacher competency has certain definite advantages.

1. A product oriented basis for competency assessment approximates a one-to-one relationship between an initial or laboratory assessment and its achievement in real teaching.

2. It represents or provides an absolute criterion of teaching effectiveness and thereby meets the ultimate test of accountability.

3. It accommodates individual differences in teaching preferences or styles by allowing for wide variation in the means of reaching a given outcome, i.e., teaching behaviors. At the same time, however, it holds all teachers accountable for being able to bring about given classes of outcomes.

4. It allows for the fact that we are not yet sure what teaching behaviors cause specific outcomes in pupils, but it does require that effective behaviors and/or instructional programs be identified and used.

5. It forces the entire educational system (not just the teacher education program) to be clear about the goals or objectives of education.

6. It will take much of the guesswork out of hiring new teachers, since each teacher will have a dossier that summarizes in detail what he can or cannot do when he receives certification.

However advantageous it may appear to base competency assessment on product criteria, it is likely that most teacher preparation programs will shift only slightly in this direction during the next decade. But we believe it likely that increasing portions of teacher preparation will be directed toward performance criteria.

Conditions Necessary for Implementation

Regardless of the basis for assessing competency, two general conditions must be met if competency based teacher preparation programs are to become a reality: (1) reasonably precise statements of the specific competencies must be made; and (2) at the same time, reliable procedures must be developed for assessing competence in terms of the appropriate criteria.

Within these general conditions, certain procedural conditions must be met if competency is to be a useful basis for the design of teacher preparation programs and for professional certification. One of the most important of these is the need for collaborative decisions on what behavior and what products are to serve as the criteria base for competency assessment. It is no longer possible or desirable for the teacher education institution to be the major determinant of either program focus or certification requirements. There are no existing precedents for choosing the most appropriate mix of agencies and/or persons to select and specify appropriate knowledge, behaviors, or product outcomes. It seems reasonable that representatives from state departments of education, professional education associations, teacher unions, citizens from associated school districts, and students themselves should join university faculties in determining what knowledge, behaviors, and product outcomes shall stand as a basis for competency assessment.

Another important condition is the need for effective use of the behavioral objective as a form for stating outcome expectancies. As long as it is remembered that there are severe limitations to the behavioral objective (e.g., it is useful in stating short-range objectives but is an awkward vehicle for dealing with outcomes that provide for a divergency of response), it can provide precision, direction, and a basis for reliable measurement.

To a certain extent, the success of competency based teacher preparation programs will be a function of educator willingness to concentrate teacher preparation efforts on relatively short-range instructional objectives. For instance, if pupils need better comprehension of what they read, achieving a specified gain in their reading comprehension is a desirable, attainable, and measurable product outcome; even though the goal has long-term significance for the pupil, gain can be attained and measured on a relatively short-term basis. On the other hand, achievement of the skills and predisposition to continue learning throughout a lifetime is a long-range objective for which short-term indicators can only be inferred. Certainly it is in no way a less important outcome than reading comprehension. Nevertheless, it is questionable whether we can hold teachers, much less prospective teachers, accountable for bringing about this outcome.

It is likely that long-range objectives will continue to be deemed highly important. Since the use of product criteria seems impractical, we must develop performance criteria in terms of reasonable hypotheses about what teacher behavior will yield desirable long-range outcomes. We can then proceed to hold prospective teachers accountable for acquiring these behavior patterns.

There is some danger in being so specific about the outcomes of instruction and the behaviors believed useful in bringing about the outcomes. Criticism of teacher education as irrelevant has always been based on speculative grounds. The lack of visible performance expectancies has protected schools from being held directly accountable for educational failures. The establishment of a competency base for teacher preparation and certification would render education vulnerable to public scrutiny. Some may find this threatening, but it could serve as a powerful regenerative force in the profession. When performance expectancies for teaching and teacher education are clearly specified, and prospective teachers are held accountable for meeting them, the credibility gap between the critic and the criticized becomes manageable.

The contexts in which competency is demonstrated are of crucial importance to teacher preparation programs. Where performance and product based criteria are concerned, context is paramount. Thus, one of the key conditions for implementing a competency based program is the provision of multiple contexts for assessment. But many context questions remain to be asked; answers must be found for such questions as:

1. In what settings will the behavior be demonstrated? In film simulated classroom settings? In microteaching situations where children are brought to an experimental classroom or laboratory? With small groups of children in ongoing classroom situations? With entire classrooms of children?

2. In how many settings should a given class of teaching behaviors be demonstrated? For example, if a student is preparing to teach at the elementary level should he demonstrate a given teaching behavior at all grade levels; for different kinds of student groups

within a sample of grade levels; or in some or all of these settings on different occasions?

3. What variation is acceptable in the performance of a given teaching behavior or in the selection of teaching behaviors to be demonstrated? Are all students in a given program expected to perform to the same criterion level on the same set of teaching behaviors? If not, who is to determine what variance is acceptable?

Similar context questions must be answered with regard to the use of product based criteria: How many times and with what kinds of children must prospective teachers demonstrate that they can bring about given classes of outcomes? If they are planning to become elementary teachers, must they demonstrate that they can bring about a given outcome for all grade levels within an elementary school? What variation in outcome demonstration can be permitted among students within a given institution or among institutions within a given state?

Consequences

The use of specifically stated competencies as a basis for teacher preparation and certification has far-reaching consequences. Among the important changes that would occur are the following:

1. Teacher preparation would become a noncourse, noncredit enterprise. Courses and credit have always been tied to a time base. Successful demonstration of competencies is in no way tied to time; in fact, it is theoretically possible to demonstrate all competencies without spending any time in an instructional program.

2. There would be a constant interplay between personal goal setting; information gathering, i.e., studying and trial teaching; and assessment of short-range outcome achievement. In other words, for the prospective teacher, competency based programs would be a highly active endeavor comprising high motivation, successive approximation of final goal behavior, and immediate knowledge of success.

3. A new range of teacher education specialists would emerge to design materials and assessment techniques and carry out actual competency assessment as described elsewhere in this volume.

4. There would be intensified efforts to clarify the nature of desirable pupil outcomes.

5. Achievement of stated educational objectives would be more likely to be attained.

Footnotes

1. See, e.g., Bruce J. Biddle & W. J. Ellena, eds., *Contemporary Research on Teacher Effectiveness* (New York: Holt, Rinehart & Winston, 1964).

5

Continuity in Teacher Education

Richard T. Coffing

James M. Cooper

Position

Preservice and inservice teacher training should be joined in teacher education systems that provide for continuous professional growth, directly related to the teacher's on-the-job performance. Competency based systems approaches should be extended to the full range of professional development from initial preparation to permanent retirement.

Rationale

A friend of ours—a television broadcast engineer and lover of high-fidelity stereophonic recordings—tells us that a common mistake made by inexperienced hi-fi owners is to put together a number of high-performance components in a system that has only mediocre audio speakers. Instead of hi-fi, they get "medium-fi." In such a system, says our friend, the audio speakers typically are "critical limiting factors."

We believe that a "critical limiting factor" in public education is the fragmented and grossly unbalanced character of teacher education programing. We are particularly concerned about the lack of a systematic interrelationship between the preservice preparation of prospective teachers and the inservice training of practicing teachers.

This limiting factor can be removed by designing and implementing an integrated, competency based systems approach to teacher education that will continually educate the teacher from the time of entry into the profession until retirement.

We have made some assumptions about teacher education, and to some extent the analysis and discussion that follows will focus on continuity as instrumental to the achievement of certain objectives. These we list without defense as among the "oughts" of teacher education programing.

1. A teacher's competence should be continuously growing with respect to given knowledge, teaching performances, and expected student outcomes.

2. The practicing teacher should have the opportunity for growth with respect to changing job requirements, whether these changing requirements are employer-initiated or self-initiated.

3. Professional learning experiences should be available to the teacher whenever they are needed.

4. The teacher should be kept informed of available educational opportunities.

5. The individual teacher, the employing school, and other "partners in teacher education" should be able to maintain an anticipatory design strategy to provide for possible future professional development needs.

Major Components of Continuity in Teacher Education

The Preservice Fragment

Traditionally, teacher education and preservice preparation were thought of as synonymous and coterminous. Teacher education programs, based in universities and colleges, were rather intensive periods of training occurring almost exclusively before a person's entry into the profession. On completion of the necessary content and professional courses, a compact period of practice, and all degree requirements, a person became a "teacher." His training was largely over, and he was considered as ready to accept the full responsibilities of teaching as his colleague in the next room, who might be starting his fourteenth year in the classroom. Teacher education programs seem to have been based on the belief that the completion of preservice training and attainment of a teaching credential created a lifetime of professional competence or that any inadequacies in a teacher's preservice training left a lifetime of irremediable professional handicaps.

Kevin Ryan of the University of Chicago tersely characterizes preservice education as "a national embarrassment. It is understaffed, under-financed and under-conceptualized. If a teacher succeeds in a classroom today, 90 percent of the credit goes to him rather than the program that trains him."[1] As B. Othanel Smith and his colleagues observe,

> A professional person is trained for and dedicated to the performance of a set of tasks within a flexible theoretical framework. But programs of teacher preparation equip the prospective teacher to perform very few specific tasks and to understand only superficially the situations he must deal with as a teacher.[2]

In presenting a rationale for new program designs, Louis J. Rubin, former director of the Center for Coordinated Education at the University of California at Santa Barbara, notes that "because of our limited understanding of the nature of teaching, and because of the great diversity of goals teachers try to accomplish with their learners, preservice training rarely enables a teacher to accomplish a specified mission with guaranteed outcomes."[3]

Whatever the effectiveness of current teacher education programs as preparation to enter the profession, their influence on the profession is likely to be blunted by the passage of time and the high dropout rate among prospective teachers, many of whom either do not enter teaching or leave the field shortly after completion of their preparation programs. Over the past decade, the proportion of formally prepared students who did not immediately enter active teaching employment has consistently been about 30 percent, and it is estimated that 50 percent of the formally prepared students are not teaching just two years after completion of their programs.

Traditional teacher education programs cannot "create a lifetime of professional competence." There is not enough time. The real world is more diverse, if not more perverse, than beginning teachers can be prepared for. Knowledge becomes obsolete; more effective methods are developed; public expectations of schools change; pupils change; teachers change; roles change.

The Inservice Fragment

We agree with the direction, though not completely with the

force, of Rubin's statement, "In the making of a teacher, it is highly probably that inservice training is infinitely more important than preservice training."[4] What is being done for the professional development of practicing teachers both in the crucial first two years and beyond? The answer as a general conclusion is "very little," although the means are now available and systematic efforts to do "very much" are beginning to be made.

Inservice education practices are still pale reflections of what they should be. Ben M. Harris and Wailand Bessent, among others, point out severe deficiencies in local staff development resources, for example, average supervisor-teacher ratios of about 1 to 100.[5]

As they do with preservice preparation, the universities and colleges maintain a virtual monopoly on continued teacher education. But, as Smith and his associates observe,

The work the teacher takes usually does not prepare him to be better at the tasks that arise on his job, or, for that matter, to perform any tasks at all. In far too many institutions, the preparation beyond his preservice training is not directed to the improvement of his performance.[6]

Inservice programs are too often inconveniently timed for the teacher. Most inservice activities or courses are conducted after school, on Saturdays, and during vacations. Moreover, financial compensation for the "overtime" required is extremely rare, aside from the credit based salary increments accruing from formal course work.

In the typical school organization today, teachers are treated as interchangeable parts (aside from subject matter divisions). Neither role definition nor compensation plan recognizes differences in tasks, levels of responsibilities, or individual capabilities. Schools that are slow to differentiate their staffing patterns are thereby missing the opportunity to design into their organization the inservice training that master or senior teachers could provide.

Continuity

"One must start," says Ted Sizer, "with the assumption that an educator is never fully educated and that, like the best of the university professors, his intellectual and practical development is a continuous thing and must be nourished regularly."[7] If we accept this assumption, it becomes apparent that our present compartmentalization of preservice and inservice education must be replaced by a view of the "intellectual and practical development" of educators as a continuum beginning with the decision to prepare for the teaching profession and ending only on retirement.

Smith and his associates introduce the notion of "perennial teacher education" with the words:

> Preparation of the teacher can begin as far down the scale of professional competence as the teacher aide, but there is no upper limit to the preparation he can have. As long as knowledge about education continues to increase and new techniques and devices are contrived, there will be something new for the teacher to learn regardless of his degree or years of experience. The continuum of preparation can therefore cover the teacher's entire career.[8]

Preservice preparation and inservice education need to be conceptualized, designed, implemented, and evaluated together. It would be better if the preservice-inservice distinction were eliminated entirely. Teacher education should be reconceptualized as an integrated continuing education system providing for continuous professional growth directly related to teaching performance requirements.

On-the-Job Performance

It might seem patently obvious that teacher education should be designed to improve teaching performance. The problem of course is the disparity between intention and action. In the past teacher education institutions have not founded their programs on the operational requirements of the real world. Relevance begins with the client's or the environment's needs; when a major client is an employing school system, the teacher education program should be designed in part to train for that client's (or class of clients') task performance requirements. In other words, its objectives should be defined in terms of knowledge, performance, and pupil outcomes expected by real schools. Of course this means that the schools, as well as teacher educators and teachers, must be involved in task analysis. And it implies different organizing principles and technologies from most current teacher education programs.

Competency Based Systems Approaches

New designs are necessary: designs technologically powerful enough to have a high probability of achieving the ends we seek. Competency based systems approaches such as those discussed in this volume offer much of the methodology for designing, operating, and evaluating teacher education systems to meet the indicated criteria.

A quick review of competency based systems approaches to teacher education shows their compatibility with the objectives that got us started on the topic of continuity.

1. The competency based approaches are deliberately designed for growth with respect to given knowledge, teaching performances, and student outcomes, because they define the possible hierarchies of learning, from the simple to the complex, in the various content and skill areas.

2. They are deliberately designed for self-renewal; as their content and processes become obsolete, the system is redesigned continuously.

3. Their design strategy calls for timely delivery of instruction, i.e., when the teacher needs it, not just during vacations, weekends, and after-hours sessions.

4. They attempt to make as explicit and as public as possible the alternative objectives and instructional routes from which the next steps of growth can be selected.

5. They include technology that enables the various partners in teacher education to maintain anticipatory design activities that permit the program to continue delivering the most relevant instruction based on changing needs.

Furthermore, competency based systems approaches offer dynamic vehicles for the teacher-learner, the training institution, and the school to assess and match their respective needs and competencies. Extended to certification agencies, the same technology can make the certification process more relevant to the actual needs of the schools.

Conditions Necessary for Implementing Continuity

The changes will be particularly crucial in two areas: institutional relationships and resource allocations.

Institutional Relationships

Organizing for continuity in teacher education will require new institutional relationships. The various parties who contribute to teacher education—the universities and colleges, school systems, state certification agencies, unions and other professional associations, industry, educational laboratories, and research and development centers—will need to be organized into partnerships that function as total systems. This means that much of the actual, or theoretical, collaboration[9] among existing institutions, which often seem to be acting independently and at cross purposes, must be incorporated into more systematic, continuous, formal organizations.

The new relationship patterns will have to be established locale by locale and region by region; the specific design of each will need to be based on the needs, resources, and constraints of its specific situation. Some will take the form of federations and consortia. Some will be patterned after the "training complex" idea introduced in *Teachers for the Real World.*[10]

The training complex is a new institutional form that undoubtedly will be implemented in a number of locales. The Office of Education has invested more than $2 million in research, development, testing, and dissemination of the concept. As described in an advisory report, a training complex will be able to

draw on the formal resources of both school and university and other professionals in practice and the informal resources of the Community (defined, alternatively, as parents, interested neighborhood agencies, industry, etc.) and which is operationally responsive to the ongoing needs of the member components, but not dominated by any single component.

Employing the strengths of the school, the university, and the community will enable training complexes to establish their own areas of responsibility: that of identifying needs and of *training* teachers and other educational personnel on a continuous basis to meet these needs.[11]

One obstacle to continuity has been the full, and often permanent, credentialing of teachers on completion of preservice preparation. Instead, the certification system should recognize the college graduate as a beginner in need of further training; initial credentials should be provisional and later credentials should be job or performance related. Such a change would certainly help blur the distinction between preservice and inservice education.

Resource Reallocation

Establishing continuous professional development will require a reallocation of expenditures. We assume that financial changes will occur as an element of changing organizational patterns, but we anticipate that the reallocation of resources will be most important and perhaps most problematic in universities and colleges on the one hand and in local school systems on the other.

We believe that university resources in the teacher education programs should be systematically shifted from the almost exclusive support of preservice preparation that now exists to a balanced expenditure over the continuum of professional development. The continued growth of practicing teachers is a critical limiting factor that must be changed if teacher education is to be substantially improved. It is economically wasteful—that is to say, it is wasteful of the considerable talents of current teacher educators—to concentrate on preparing preservice teachers, so many of whom will shortly leave or never enter the profession, and virtually ignore the systematic continuing education needs of teachers in the first crucial years of teaching and in the years of potential growth thereafter.

Another crucial locus for change in resource allocation is certainly the local school system; there, political and economic problems are more difficult than in the university or college. In general, it can be said that current local expenditures for continuing education are miniscule in relation to the need. Much more of the local expenditure for education should be devoted to continued professional development of the teaching staff.

The major problems in local reallocation of funds to professional development are considerable. Overall budgets are severely limited: a trend that is increasing. Qualified professional development staff are in short supply, although we believe that limitation is diminishing. But we suspect that the knottiest problem has to do with the obsolete notions that the individual teacher should be almost solely responsible for his own professional growth and that institutions should support professional growth only through the modest, credit based reward system. Again, one of the most promising solutions is to differentiate the staff and incorporate integrated systems of continuing education as a major commitment in the new organization.

Consequences

In general, establishing continuity would eliminate a "critical limiting factor": the fragmentation and grossly unbalanced character of teacher education programing.

Benefits

With continuity, we think teachers would be able to satisfy their personal professional needs more completely than has been possible. They would be able to update their personal inventory of objectives and competencies continuously. Furthermore, they would know more precisely what competencies prospective employers were seeking and would be able to select well in advance the kind of role for which they wished to prepare.

Similarly, school systems would be much more specific about their needs and would be able to communicate these needs clearly, not only to prospective teachers and staff desiring new roles, but also to the many other clients of the schools: students, parents, taxpayers, industry, and so forth. School systems would be more responsive to changing community demands, and the process would be smoother than the "stair-step" or "pendulum" change profiles more common in the past.

Continuous professional growth of teachers would contribute to the renewal of the schools. With continuous growth programing, fewer unprepared teachers would drop out because they were given no help in adapting and learning to cope with realities of the classroom. Fewer capable persons would leave the profession. Teacher turnover, which now deprives schools of experienced staff, would be supplanted by a mobility that would contribute to the variety and constant renewal of public education. Reducing the teacher dropout problem would reduce the economic cost of teacher preparation, thus freeing more funds for application to continued professional growth.

Presented with a clearer picture of the professional activities in a teaching career, more persons who should not become teachers would transfer out of teacher education earlier than in previous years. Similarly, more persons who should be teachers would be attracted to teaching.

With continuity as we define it, the methods of training the beginner and the experienced teacher would be consistent, thus enhancing the power of education for both. Moreover, the institutional partners in education and teacher training would operate on better data about the real needs and desires of all learners—"teachers" as well as "students"—in the system.

Other Results

The consequences of establishing continuity may not all be beneficial. Eliminating one critical limiting factor in a system usually means that some other factor becomes critical. For example, if teachers experienced continuous professional growth, the critical factor might become the funds appropriated for employing new teachers to keep up with population growth. If these funds were insufficient, the system would be unbalanced in another way.

In some places continuity might be achieved only in the form of a rigid, unresponsive curriculum. Such a teacher education program might be called a "whole," but it would become increasingly irrelevant to the changing needs of school children.

Finally, referring to the analogy of the hi-fi stereo components, it will always be necessary to ask, even of the integrated system of continuing education, "All right, now that we have a better balanced, high-fidelity system, what should we be listening to?" Answering that question requires the crossing of disciplinary boundaries at all levels, and that is the central concern of the following chapter.

Footnotes

1. Kevin Ryan (Address to the Regional Conference, Study of the Comprehensive High School in Massachusetts, sponsored by the Massachusetts Advisory Council on Education, April 10, 1970).

2. B. Othanel Smith, Saul E. Cohen & Arthur Pearl, *Teachers for the Real World*, (Washington, D.C.: American Assoc. of Colleges for Teacher Education, 1969), p. 24.

3. Louis J. Rubin, *A Study on the Continuing Education of Teachers* (Santa Barbara: Center for Coordinated Education, University of California, 1969), p. 4.

4. Ibid.

5. Ben M. Harris & Wailand Bessent, *In-service Education: A Guide to Better Practice* (Englewood Cliffs, N.J.: Prentice-Hall, 1969), p. 7.

6. Smith, Cohen & Pearl, *Teachers for the Real World*, p. 153.

7. National Education Association, *Remaking the World of the Career Teacher* (Washington, D.C.: NCTEPS, National Education Assoc., 1966), p. 14.

8. Smith, Cohen & Pearl, *Teachers for the Real World*, p. 151.

9. E. Brooks Smith, Hans C. Olsen, Patrick J. Johnson & Chandler

Barbour, eds., *Partnership in Teacher Education* (Washington, D.C.: American Assoc. of Colleges for Teacher Education, 1968).

10. Smith, Cohen & Pearl, *Teachers for the Real World,* pp. 95–109.

11. Saul B. Cohen & Mitchell P. Lichtenberg, eds., *Final Report of the Ad Hoc National Advisory Committee on Training Complexes* (Worcester, Mass.: Clark University, 1970), p. 7.

6
Teacher Education as Interdisciplinary Study

W. Robert Houston

J. Bruce Burke

Position

Teacher education is coming of age as a behavioral science. The 1970s will see teacher education programs developed and conducted on the basis of empirical knowledge about human learning and the conditions best suited to effect it. Teacher education programs will make a systematic contribution to this empirical base as a new environment of systems planned, competency based programs contributes to controlled research. The thesis of this chapter is that these new teacher education programs must be interdisciplinary in approach. We believe this is necessary for two basic reasons: (1) the behavioral sciences are interdisciplinary by nature, and (2) teaching tasks call on such a wide range of sensitivities, information, and skills that only an interdisciplinary approach can adequately prepare teachers.

Rationale

Emergence of Behavioral Science

The scientist in the twentieth century has achieved an unparalleled prestige. To many he is the modern day incarnation of Plato's Philosopher King. Some imagine the scientist is an authority on all subjects, a mystic seer who holds the key to the solution of the vital questions of survival. Much of the public adulation of the scientist is pure superstition in contemporary garb, but one must admit the scientist's role in our society is pivotal. His accumulated information, methodology in problem solving, broad theoretical base, and advanced technological tools for data gathering and analyzing have all made revolutionary contributions to today's world; such contributions continue expanding in geometric progression.

Achievements in the sciences of human behavior, however, have been less than spectacular. One reason is that the empirical study of the physical world has had a long history, while the systematic study of man is of comparatively recent origin. Man investigated astronomy before geography, physics before biology, and zoology before psychology. This last frontier, the study of man, is the domain of the behavioral sciences.

By behavioral sciences we mean inquiries—both methods and findings—that constitute reliable and valid sources of empirical information about man's nature and condition. The behavioral sciences are eclectic; they cut across established disciplines to focus on basic empirical knowledge about the activities of man. Of special interest to the behavioral scientist are such disciplines as psychology, sociology, anthropology, political science, communications, and economics; interdisciplines such as social psychology; and various subdisciplines, such as cognitive development, cultural anthropology, and linguistics.

The energetic activities of the behavioral sciences sometimes generate spectacular results; often, however, these results are lost in a sea of meaningless jargon and conflicting opinion. There are few if any unifying theories in the behavioral sciences of the magnitude of those proposed by Newton, Descartes, Darwin, or Einstein in the natural sciences. Newton wrote, "If I have seen a little farther than others, it is because I have stood on the shoulders of giants." There is no comparable tradition yet in the behavioral sciences. However, the behavioral sciences already have made impressive contributions to a knowledge base for the development of teacher education.

The identification and quantification of significant variables is a necessary prerequisite to theory building. The development of ancient astronomy is a particularly striking example of this. From the beginning of serious study by the Babylonians in 700 B.C. to the writing of Ptolemy's *Almagest* 850 years later, students of astronomy considered which variables should be measured, recorded, and retained. Theory could not advance until observations began to accumulate. Ptolemy's comprehensive mathematical synthesis of this long tradition relied on observations and measurements dating back hundreds of years. As we study and formulate hypotheses about human behavior, however, we seldom remember that progress in the natural sciences has also been tortuous and slow.

Empirical researchers first studied man from isolated and often insulated viewpoints. Initial efforts to study human behavior focused on the psychological man, the sociological man, the anthropological man, or the communicating man. Results were often limited because of the restricted vision of the researchers; their observations were like the blind men's descriptions of the elephant as a wall, tree trunk, or rope, depending on their limited contact. The early work of learning theorists virtually ignored the work of sociologists. But when culture, social context, and environmental forces were included in research designs, several important findings emerged. Still other insights about learning are developing as a result of the interaction of psychology and human medicine. The discovery of the relation of proteins to learning and of protein deficiency in early childhood to learning disabilities is an example of the potential of interdisciplinary investigations. New insights are gained when inquiry methods of one discipline are focused on the problems of another. If we are ever to make important strides, we must use the talents and resources of several disciplines to examine human behavior.

Recently teams of behavioral scientists representing various disciplines have begun to examine major social problems. As systematic interrelationships are explored in more detail, the possibilities for more comprehensive theories of behavior are enhanced. As theories of behavior become more comprehensive and we can explain and predict behavioral outcomes in situations with many biological, psychological, and cultural variables, behavior theory will become still more useful.

Teacher Education as a Behavioral Science

Professional teacher education is itself an interdisciplinary study. From the behavioral sciences it draws content and modes of inquiry for understanding human behavior. It applies these concepts not only to the content of its own program, but also to the processes of teacher education.

On the surface a behavioral view of teaching and teachers

appears to be more concerned with what the teacher *does* than with what the teacher *is.* Deeper analyses, however, establish relationships between what the teacher does and the causes of his behavior; thus a behavioral view of teaching is concerned with the person of the teacher, his value system, and his affective biases and the influence of these variables on his teaching behaviors.

Inquiry into the roots and consequences of teaching behaviors constitutes a valid exercise for both the researching behavioral scientist and the student of behavioral science. The scientist's main goal is the development of a conceptual structure; the teacher's goals are client related. The two goals are intertwined in the teacher education program. Certain techniques and attitudes of inquiry that characterize the several behavioral sciences are useful to the teacher and can be learned by prospective teachers. On the other hand, the context of the school and the roles of the teacher can be laboratories for developing new methods of studying behavior and refining theories. A major responsibility of teacher education programs is to use these evolving theories, knowledges, and constructs; it must also contribute to their further development and refinement.

Theoretical activity evolves from experience and leads directly back into practice. Problems are studied, described, and analyzed; hypotheses are proposed; action is taken; and evidence is sought on the consequences of the action. On the basis of data from the latter evaluation, revised problem situations are considered. This paradigm for action is useful for the behavioral researcher, the elementary teacher, and the developers of teacher education programs. It illustrates another interrelationship among persons concerned with human behavior: a system in which each party contributes to a better understanding of the whole.

Conditions for Implementing an Interdisciplinary Approach in Teacher Education

Viewing teacher education as a behavioral science, we believe the content must be interdisciplinary. Part of the reason is that a variety of scientific disciplines—e.g., pyschology, sociology, anthropology, and linguistics—constitute the field of behavioral studies. The more fundamental reason is that teacher education aims at producing a professional teacher whose skills and knowledge cut across the traditional boundaries of the academic disciplines. A compartmentalized view of life is useful to the academic scholar extending the frontiers of knowledge in increasingly narrow specialties. Outside of university departments and professional associations, however, life is experienced as a whole. The teacher needs the multiple skills that come from a pluralistic learning environment in order to match the pluralism of the classroom.

The Role of Academic Disciplines

The interdisciplinary approach to teacher education acknowledges the contribution of the academic disciplines but seeks to go beyond them to obtain the insights that emerge when the disciplinary lines of investigation intersect. It is on this point that James Conant failed to comprehend the full potential of interdisciplinary studies in teacher education. Conant wrote that "collegiate faculties should define the levels of knowledge and understanding or skill that should be required of the total general education of the future teacher."[1] There is the musty smell of the traditional scholar's faith in an intellectual *noblesse oblige* in this distastefully patronizing view that experts can set standards for education by adding up the academicians' accumulated wisdom. Conant did not explain that the sum of a potential teacher's insights is greater than the parts or pieces of knowledge, information, and facts received from the several disciplines. Wisdom can be achieved only by the integration of knowledge, the synthesizing of information, and the correlation of truths in the minds of individual students.

It is not an interdisciplinary approach to get scholars working side by side to develop curricula. What is needed is an intensive *mixture* of disciplines with professors working as a team before students to focus on problems, concepts, and themes that cut across their various disciplines. This is not easy; over time each discipline has built high walls of language, attitudes, skills, and knowledge to distinguish it from its nearest competitors. In this fight for identity the disciplines have lost contact with other fields. "Professors of various academic departments," writes Stiles, "guard the sanctity of their disciplines with a devotion that tolerates few deviations."[2]

The Student as an Integrating Element

The problems facing future teachers are integrated problems

that cannot be solved by disintegrating skills. Moreover, the contemporary student asks for more meaning in his analysis of the world than a single discipline can offer. This is one way, at least, to interpret what students mean by their demands for "relevance" in their course of study. William Arrowsmith sums up this problem and recommends an interdisciplinary approach. He writes that the scholar's

comparative security, his cosy enclave of learning with its narrow departmental limits, and his murderous preference for a single mode of the mind—the discursive or methodological, do not call it "rational"—with its neat problems and solutions, his studied humanity—all this strikes the student as irrelevant and even repugnant. What he wants is models of committed integrity, as whole as they can be in a time of fragmented men. Admittedly such models are hard to find, and integrated men are not to be expected. Hence it is essential that a student be confronted with as many *different* vivid modes as we can muster; from these he may be able to infer the great, crucial idea of all true education—the single, many sided transformation of himself, the man he wants to be.[3]

General education for teachers should not be defined as a collection of courses in "subjects," or as a set of skills or facts, as Conant would recommend. It is a set of experiences that should be designed to open the mind, enlarge the spirit, and challenge the powers of the total personality. Different people have different needs and must involve themselves in different learning tasks. Again, Arrowsmith makes the point well. "What we must have, unless we are prepared to abandon our fate to parochial technicians, is precisely the pluralism to which we are committed. We need *options,* choices, alternatives; we need to honor the diversity of human skills and needs."[4] Thus, if the objective of general education is the development of persons, a wide variety of opportunities must be available to them, not a narrowly constrained curriculum.

To take an interdisciplinary approach in the education of teachers is to emphasize the role of the student in the process of discovery. Marshall McLuhan reminds us that in *Science and the Modern World* Alfred North Whitehead pointed out that the great discovery of the latter nineteenth century was not the invention of this or that, but the discovery of the technique of discovery. "We can discover anything we decide to discover."[5] The individual student's interaction with the methods of a variety of disciplines in a search for solutions to problems requires that each student participate in the process of discovery. Once learned, this process is applicable to any set of problems. An interdisciplinary approach promotes student participation, because no single professor or discipline can pose as the final authority. It permits us to discard the pretense of "covering the material"—the so-called blanket theory of general education—when the material turns out to be a question of man's ecological survival or of securing peace for the world.

The Team Approach

A team approach is implied in constructing an interdisciplinary curriculum. It is the mixture of expertise we seek, but even more crucial is the example of knowledgeable men teaching each other, learning from each other, and thus providing a model of cooperative interaction for students. A professor on an interdisciplinary team admits his finite knowledge, shows his willingness to learn, and shares with the students the process of discovery. These benefits accrue even when a single professor teaches a course designed by an interdisciplinary team. We have discovered that students respond with enthusiasm more often when we struggle with them in fields unfamiliar to us both. It was a blow to the ego to find that when we dealt at length and with precision on the subjects within an interdisciplinary course about which we felt knowledgeable, students turned strangely restless and willing to "take an expert's word." Something exciting happens when professor and students grow together in exploring unfamiliar fields. The point is not that we need less knowledgeable professors, but that students need to have us move our expertise out of their way.

Demands of a Rapidly Evolving Culture

Our cultural patterns are changing so rapidly that the traditional disciplines, which have a long history of development from the medieval university, no longer provide an adequate base for analyzing contemporary human experience. Our images of man are changing, and many believe we must no longer pose questions about Man, *sub species aeternalis,* but speak of people. Fourteen years ago Lynn White, Jr., wrote that "one talks about people, about the ways in which they act and interact, think and feel in terms of the pattern of a given culture, and about how deviation from the norms of that culture molds individuals and eventually may remold the pattern of culture." [6] White's hypothesis is that the very canons of our culture are shifting. The canon of the West is being displaced by the canon of the globe. The canons of logic and language are being expanded by the canon of symbols; the canon of rationality is being supplemented by the canon of the unconscious; and the canon of the hierarchy of values is giving way to the canon of the spectrum of values.[7] The accuracy of White's analysis is remarkable in view of the fact that his observations were made more than a decade ago. Our times confirm a cultural upheaval along the lines he described. Students today seek a process for discovering who they are in terms of a global world, a variety of symbols and values, and their awareness of the power of the unconscious. Nothing less than an interdisciplinary approach even comes close to responding to that search.

Experience with Interdisciplinary Efforts

Attempts to develop interdisciplinary approaches to education are found in abundance at such universities as Chicago, Utah, Columbia, Berkeley, and Michigan State. To some extent each attempt has failed. Many of these failures may have been caused by the tendency to establish a fixed curriculum instead of a constantly changing one that can adapt to real issues. The world changes so rapidly that today's relevance is tomorrow's irrelevance, and any static coalition of disciplines or curriculum experiences is inert from the outset and remains a sterile tribute to yesterday.

The old humanism failed because it did not adapt to new and emerging missions. Scholasticism was repudiated when it became rigid and deaf to the issues of the day; a once progressive philosophy had become a dogma. In previous eras change occurred far more slowly than today; it took decades, even centuries, to get rid of an irrelevant system. This is no longer the case, and interdisciplinary efforts will adapt more readily to the needs of the present and future when professors observe the past as prologue rather than prescription.

The Educational Experience of the Prospective Teacher

A major component of the prospective teacher's education is the development of skills for analyzing human behavior. However, this is not the only phase of his preparation that requires the resources of several disciplines. A prospective teacher is, first and foremost, a person; he must be respected as an individual personality.

Secondly, he is a knowing person, a problem-solving person, a person employing the knowledge and modes of inquiry of many disciplines in addition to the behavioral sciences. His preparation should be designed to sharpen his skills for understanding human behavior, but it should also provide the needed resources for analyzing other kinds of problems. This is vital if we assume the teacher's approach to problem solving will have a significant impact on pupil problem-solving techniques.

The Teacher as Individual

The teacher's effectiveness depends to a great extent on his possession of those sympathetic and generous qualities that make him humane. His interaction with others, understanding of their needs, and empathy with their problems depend on the person behind the professional. In fact, a teacher's professionalism must be measured in terms of these qualities. We question any claim that professional skill in reading, for example, can be developed in isolation from the growth of the humane consideration of a child's individual needs. Thus, a primary concern in teacher education is the cultivation of sensitivity.

A broad informational base is not sufficient for effective instruction. If it were, computers would be our best teachers, for we could in time store the knowledge of the ages within their memory banks. "The advancement of learning at the expense of man," warned Nietzsche, "is the most pernicious thing in the world." This implies that there are different ways of learning: one way stunts our growth with the burden of knowledge for its own sake; another way promotes our expansion as human beings with knowledge that serves us. Melby made this point when he wrote:

We have assumed that the educated man is one who *knows;* yet *knowing* about literature may give one little sense of human tragedy or of belonging to humanity, little compassion. Knowing some science—let us say physics—may do little to help one sense the spirit of science. If we really believe in a liberal education, we must be more concerned with what students are and are becoming than with what they know and are learning in fact and skill. This does not mean that knowledge is unimportant but rather that the true teacher sees knowledge as a means, not as an end. [8]

Education in general, and teacher education in particularly, will fail to achieve its objective if it is reduced to skill development;

knowledge stuffing; or mechanical manipulation of variables, either scientific or human. A sense of perspective, a feeling for the integrity of individuals, and a positive attitude toward the human potential for growth are vital characteristics of a mature person and a professional teacher.

One way to develop these human qualities in the prospective teacher is to apply an interdisciplinary approach to the study of foreign cultures. It takes great sensitivity to develop the ability to stand in another's cultural shoes. Intensive exposure to the thought, institutions, art, and literature of other countries—particularly non-western cultures—can lessen cultural biases and broaden sensitivity to the valid differences between peoples. The mixture of liberal studies, e.g., in philosophy, the fine arts, and literature, with the more pragmatic concerns of the social sciences can bring about an integrated experience for the prospective teacher.

The comparative study of cultures in a college or through direct experience in foreign countries can help the prospective teacher understand himself and his own values. Through the recognition of differing and often conflicting values in other cultures, he can better understand differing values within his own culture. A major cause of teaching failure by teachers of inner-city youngsters is the conflict between the teachers' values and those of the children. Certainly the prospective teacher cannot recognize his pupils as persons unless he himself has been accorded that status and has developed a consciousness of and respect for himself as a person.

The Teacher as Problem Solver

To what end do we study, store facts and concepts, and develop ever more refined techniques for analysis? One pragmatic reason is to solve problems and make decisions. The problem may be which television program to watch, how to settle an argument between children, or which job to take or house to buy. Or the problem may be a far-reaching one: environmental pollution; population growth; the effects of cybernation; social dichotomies, e.g., between young and old, white and nonwhite, and haves and have-nots; or the deterioration of cities. These are some of the problems we face today; they are real to the younger generation. The larger issues have been long in the making and will be complex in solution. Certainly the solutions of these problems require an interdisciplinary approach, but so do our more mundane problems.

By placing the relevant problems of the moment at the center of an interdisciplinary field of study, a prospective teacher can learn a process of problem solving that is applicable to any set of problems. It is this characteristic of learning that produces permanence and coherence in interdisciplinary studies.

Consequences

The implications of an interdisciplinary concept of teacher education are many and far ranging. Some of them are:

1. Courses that emphasize psychology or sociology alone will disappear from the teacher education curriculum. Instead students will study the more comprehensive behavioral sciences. The constrained and compartmentalized approach to studying human behavior will be replaced by one employing the broadest possible range of concepts and modes of inquiry.

2. Joint appointments between academic departments and education will become the rule rather than the exception. Scholars from several fields will work together to develop programs suited to a wide range of students' talents and needs.

3. The reward system of the university will be broadened so that academicians can work with educational problems while receiving the acclaim of their colleagues. Indeed the concept of "colleagues" will be so altered as to encompass persons from a number of fields of study rather than a single discipline.

4. Present organizational structures and traditional approaches will not suffice to effect the interdisciplinary transformation. On many college campuses, the growing edge is not in traditional departments, but in centers, institutes, bureaus, or laboratories where scholars of various persuasions and disciplines combine their talents to solve a set of problems or a common problem. Cross-fertilization is the key to their success. These new alignments, fluid in concept and action, are designed to enhance change, not to guard the old ways. We doubt that such organizational units should ever become institutionalized; they should grow, fulfill their purposes, and dissolve. They must not become possessive of their mission or their methods, for in so doing, they will become less able to respond to new needs and new orders.

5. Professional education and general liberal education may become so intertwined as to be inseparable. For example, students might study the content of science, experiment on their own with scientific ideas, work with curriculum materials currently used by elementary pupils, and actually engage in limited instructional experience, all either concurrently or in tightly wound spirals of experience. The educational program thus would be expanded beyond the bounds of the college campus to include elementary schools. But experience in living in a foreign land, travel, or work in community projects would also replace the ivory tower concept of university learning in favor of a more global context for learning.

6. A school or division of personal services can follow from the approach taken above. Such a school would include as students social workers, urban affairs specialists, nurses, and sociologists, as well as educators. In this context they could learn to recognize the relationship between their role as teacher and the needs of the total society. They should perceive both the student role and the teaching role as parts of a set of interacting roles within the community.

7. Major aspects of the curriculum will focus on important contemporary problems that cross traditional disciplinary demarcations in their scope and solution. Faculty-student teams will work together in focusing on an issue. Experience in the *process* of problem solving is the goal.

8. The source and selection of curriculum components will involve not only the university faculty, but also the individual student. Furthermore, practicing teachers, community representatives, and social service representatives all have important contributions to make when the knowledge base is broadened and becomes a major objective. Practicing teachers, for example, might periodically participate in preservice program development and review, becoming part of teaching-learning teams. While contributing to the program, they can draw from it to improve and update their own skills of analyzing human behavior.

9. Empirical research must become an integral function in teacher education if programs are to become more effective. Such research will be comprehensive in scope and conception. Doctoral dissertations will be part of more inclusive studies rather than isolated and limited.

10. Students in an interdisciplinary problem-solving curriculum

must learn to cope with inconsistencies and ambiguities; they must be prepared to work within an open-ended discovery process. Faculty must also learn to work in fluid situations where they are at times students instead of teachers.

11. The personal preferences of the prospective teacher will be respected in the educational process. The range of alternative programs will match the range of individual differences among people.

The interdisciplinary approach thus frees educational institutions and individuals to select from alternatives. This approach must not become a static haven for those who defend the status quo; nor can it be a refuge for those who choose anonymity to conceal their deficiencies. The strength of an interdisciplinary approach to teacher education resides in its capacity to focus many skills on complex problems. Only through such a process can teacher education change and meet the needs of a changing society.

We have suggested the need for technological support throughout these pages. The optimum use of instructional technology is essential. The role of technology in facilitating the transition to a fully implemented interdisciplinary approach is discussed in the following chapter.

Footnotes

1. James B. Conant, *The Education of American Teachers* (New York: McGraw-Hill, 1963), pp. 94–95.

2. Lindley J. Stiles, "Interdisciplinary Accountability for Teacher Education," *Journal of Higher Education* (January 1968): pp. 23–31.

3. William Arrowsmith, "The Future of Teaching," *Arion* (1967): p. 11.

4. Ibid., p. 22.

5. Marshall McLuhan, *Hot and Cool* (New York: New American Library, Signet, 1967).

6. Lynn White, Jr., *Frontiers of Knowledge* (New York: Harper & Bros., 1956), pp. 301–302.

7. Ibid., pp. 302–316.

8. Ernest O. Melby, "The Contagion of Liberal Education," *Journal of Teacher Education* 18 (Summer 1967): p. 135.

7
Instructional Technology: Process and Product

Walter Dick

Norman R. Dodl

Position

The conception of technology as a laborsaving, people displacing phenomenon has done more to impede instructional improvement than has a lack of suitable educational devices. In order to overcome this conception, one must accept the notion that technology represents not only an end product in terms of hardware devices, but also, and more importantly, a systematic process for developing total educational programs and instructional materials. In order to enhance significantly the preparation of teachers, we must adopt the process of technology, which implies decisions about the most efficient uses of man and machine in order to implement a total instructional program.

What we call "technological process" is more commonly known as "instructional systems technology." In simplest terms, this use of technology implies systematic design, implementation, and assessment of both the process and the products of instruction. It involves the systematic development of sets of learning experiences that enable a learner to move step by step toward his goal, provision of contexts for assessing learning outcomes, and provision for feedback so that results can effect revision of the total system. In more complex and extensive uses of the technological process, systematic procedures are used to implement and manage the instructional system.

Rationale

Behavioral Research

Training programs of the Second World War influenced many of the current planners in educational design and development. Three who were most influenced were Skinner, Gagné, and Glaser. They were trained as experimental psychologists and had used animals—primarily rats—in basic research on psychological processes before the war. During the war they turned their intellectual energies to practical training problems.

One outcome of this experience was the realization that to train a man for a job it was necessary to know what a man in that position would actually do in the field. The result of this realization was the development of job analysis procedures. These job analyses were subsequently reduced to functional statements clearly resembling what we now call "behavioral objectives." Instructional systems were designed to produce men who could perform the functions described in the statements. One further element was included to meet the needs of the military. Men were evaluated as they functioned in the field, and this information was analyzed and used to revise the instructional program; thus, each succeeding generation of trainees was more effective than the last.

After the war Skinner, Gagné, and Glaser returned to institutions of higher education and resumed their research in the area of learning. However, they began to focus more and more attention on the area of human learning. In 1954, Skinner wrote his first article on teaching machines. His work was a response to the need to analyze the tasks a child must actually perform in order to learn mathematics. He developed an instructional technique whereby the child was given the opportunity to respond frequently and receive feedback on the accuracy of this response. This marked the beginning of the programed instruction movement.

By 1958 both Gagné and Glaser were using Skinner's programing techniques to investigate human learning under more controlled conditions. Glaser continued in this research and established the Learning Research and Development Center in Pittsburgh, which has sponsored the development of Individually Prescribed Instruction (IPI). In 1965 Gagné published *Conditions of Learning,* which has shaped both educational and psychological thinking about the learning process.

Systems Technology

Other behavioral scientists have incorporated the ideas of Skinner, Gagné, and Glaser in an "instructional systems technology." These systems incorporate job or task analysis, identification of initial skills of learners, specification of learning outcomes, and continuous system revision. This type of technological process underlies the design of many new program models for teacher education.

Why has educational technology become so influential in recent years? The impact of sometimes contradictory societal concerns demands procedures that can bring institutions into closer alignment with the heterogenous society they serve. Instructional systems technology seems to be such a procedure.

Personalization

The humanistically oriented segment of society is concerned about personalizing the total educational process. This concern is reflected in chapter 3. There has been extremely rapid growth at all levels of our educational system in recent years. One response to growth has been to assemble learners into manageable groups for formal education. But this organizational device has led to increasing charges of depersonalization in the educational process. The larger and more numerous the groups, the more difficult it is for an educational system to be responsive to individual differences.

Today, the "silent generation" of the fifties has been replaced by the "activist generation" of the sixties and seventies. Greater mobility and integration have produced greater heterogeneity among and within groups. If personalization can be achieved in education, it must start in the education of teachers. This will require programs that provide learners with a choice of goals, learning experiences, and assessment contexts and allow for individual motivations and learning rates. Individualized instruction must become a reality in teacher education before it can benefit the total educational community.

Accountability

Increasing demands from many levels of society for governmental and educational accountability are forcing adaptation of technology to teacher education. Governments at all levels are be-coming aware that society cannot afford even the present, imper-fect education system. It is not unusual for a state government to spend between 70 and 80 percent of its total income for education. Since local and state tax sources have been tapped to their limit for education funds, the federal government has begun making more sizable contributions to the educational system. Because of the increased participation by state and federal governments, responsible politicians are beginning to raise questions about the effectiveness of tax supported education. The politician is publicly accountable for the decisions he makes, and he is now asking that educators become accountable for their decisions. If the responsible educator at any level is to communicate the effectiveness of his system, he must be able to (1) state precisely what outcomes the system is designed to facilitate and (2) present evidence that the outcomes have in fact been produced.

The task now is to design programs that provide personalized and individualized instruction for large numbers of learners. At the same time these programs will be responsible for preparing teachers who can demonstrate their competence according to publicly ac-cepted criteria. Moreover, these diverse ends must be achieved within the constraint of the finite tax dollar. Technology can help meet the demands of this situation within the financial constraints.

Role Definition

Man's Role

If we accept the use of systems technology as the basis for instructional design and implementation in teacher education, it then becomes important to decide what roles are best filled by man and what is more efficiently accomplished by technological products. In terms of the original process model, it appears man must play the dominant role in all original system development. All material and strategies will be devised by man. When the system is in operation, the complexity and size of the learner population will determine the extent of man's role in managing the instructional process. Whatever the size of the system, it becomes ever more likely that management by exception will be applied to the instructional process in teacher education. In other words, intervention will be needed at points where the system ceases to function as designed. In teacher education, this might mean counseling students who are not achieving at a rate or level appropriate to their personalized profile or revising instructional materials to make them more effective. In addition, at this point man himself could be an integral instructional component within the total system. For instance, he may be needed as an evaluator of certain performances, as an interpreter of records, or as a respondent to a student seeking human assistance.

Instructional Devices; Computers

Devices such as television, radio, films, and audio tapes are being used in public schools today. Each device has features that extend the capabilities of an instructional system; however, each has generally been used only as a substitute for man in disseminating information. The student is too often considered a nonresponsive consumer of information. Given the concept of a responsive learner who questions, applies, and creates with the information supplied, these devices take on a new importance within the instructional system.

The latest and perhaps most controversial technological device being applied to education is the computer. The computer cannot be considered in the same category with television, films, audio tapes, etc., because it can control these devices and execute man-made decision algorithms. This recent innovation in educational hardware lends itself to the programing of instruction. Programing must be responsive to the learner; it must not treat him as a passive consumer. This use of technology leads to a high level of interaction between an active learner and the resources of instruction.

If we accept the premises that expenditures for education cannot continue to expand at the present rate and that there must be further exploration of the roles of technology and human ability in instructional systems, the potential of the computer must be considered further. What can a computer provide in an individualized performance based curriculum? There are at least five functions the computer could perform in the teacher training program. These functions must be designed, developed, and monitored by humans, and they could be carried out by humans. However, the computer can do it more effectively and, over the long run, more cheaply. Briefly, these functions are:

1. Computer-Managed Instruction (CMI). In this application of computers, the student does all his learning in noncomputerized modes, using texts, film strips, videotapes, lectures, discussions, and other means to learn the skills and behaviors for a specific task. When he feels he has mastered the task, he goes to an instructional computer terminal for a testlike dialogue. The computer determines whether the student has achieved the objectives for the task. If he has not, the computer recommends specific remedial activities. If he has done well, certain enrichment materials may be suggested. The computer generates one or more records of the student's performance on magnetic tapes or disks.

2. Computer-Assisted Instruction (CAI). Certain learning activities that can best be taught through drill and practice or simulation experiences may be taught directly at a computer terminal. This is the mode of instruction that has been used most often in computer research in the past, and it may be the most effective means of insuring mastery of certain knowledge outcomes in the shortest period of time. While it is costly at present, the cost will certainly be reduced in the future.

3. Scheduling. In a complex individualized instructional program, human and technological resources must be made available at appropriate times so that learning can proceed without interruption. The computer can schedule resources to achieve this end. For example, some materials, such as textbooks, may be available as needed in a resource center. However, videotaping equipment, computer terminals, instructors, space for group learning, and other scarce resources will have to be closely scheduled. Therefore, the student should be able to go directly to a computer terminal to schedule his use of resources as much as a week in advance. This will keep the manager of the training program informed about the load on various devices and the location of bottlenecks.

4. Counseling. One feature of an individualized instructional program will be the redirection of faculty efforts so that faculty can work with many more students, individually or in small groups. Routine counseling, for example, may be provided by the computer. It has already been demonstrated that academic counseling can be handled this way in a junior college. The computer provides the

student with the rules and regulations of the institution, the components of the training program, and his academic achievement to date. It could also indicate the areas yet to be covered and the requirements for those areas. This level of counseling can be done most effectively by the computer because it eliminates the human error that sometimes nullifies counseling discussions.

5. Record Keeping and Research. Because the student will be continually interacting with the computer in terms of CMI, CAI, counseling, or scheduling, the computer will have a continuous record of his progress and achievements in the curriculum. This information may be used collectively to counsel the student and manage his instructional program. Likewise the computer can record and analyze great volumes of data pertaining to the total instructional program. This information can be used by curriculum developers to improve the curriculum.

The computer is certainly the most powerful device presently available for use in the management of teacher education programs, and its effective use will be a challenge for years to come. For complex programs that serve large numbers of students, use of the computer may be the only effective and efficient way of carrying out many of the ideas expressed in this book.

Conditions Necessary for Implementation

In order to make use of educational technology in the type of individualized teacher education program described in this book, it will be necessary to develop four basic types of resources: (1) materials, (2) hardware, (3) physical facilities, and (4) human resources.

Materials

In considering the implementation of an individualized instructional program, the first reaction invariably is, "What shall I use for instructional materials?" Many of the materials available today were not designed to be independent instructional devices, nor were they designed to specify the intended outcomes of the instruction. We need a variety of instructional materials with specified learning outcomes and a defined set of procedures to evaluate these outcomes.

It is easy to see the need for such materials; it is quite another thing to develop them. Faculty members typically have not been trained to develop materials in accordance with technological procedures. In fact many of our programs have no stated objectives; thus, we cannot select suitable materials. It has been suggested that college of education faculties should work with the publishing industry to produce materials for many colleges. We predict it will require a great deal of time for education and industry to develop such productive relationships. In the meantime, it may be important to consider the role of graduate students in the production of such materials. More and more educational institutions are developing students who consider themselves "instructional technologists." Such students form an invaluable resource pool of individuals who could work with various faculty members to produce materials for individualized programs. The development of "instructional modules" now underway on a wide scale is an example of the materials development process suggested here.

Hardware

Sesame Street demonstrates the impact television can have on young children. Similar materials must be made available for teacher trainees. Current devices for viewing videotapes are bulky and expensive, but electronic video recording (EVR) systems, which permit the user to play a videotape cartridge in a conventional television set, will soon be on the market at a reasonable cost. There is a similar need for the development of relatively inexpensive computer systems specifically geared to meet the needs of education. In addition to developing functional applications for computers, we must pursue further research into the development of inexpensive terminal devices.

Facilities

Colleges considering individualized programs have realized that their physical facilities are almost totally inappropriate for such innovative programs. These programs call for individual learning carrels with multimedia devices at hand, small conference rooms, videotaping and viewing facilities, evaluation centers for teachers and small groups of students, and large learning resource centers. Almost none of these facilities are available in colleges built more than ten years ago. Such colleges have an abundance of thirty- to fifty-student classrooms, which are of little or no value in an individualized program. Therefore, colleges will have to follow the lead of public schools in developing such architectural concepts as pods and individual study facilities.

Human Resources

The final and the most important consideration in the implementation of instructional technology is the effective use of the limited human resources available. Faculty members who are to be involved in the development of new programs must be convinced of the need to develop a new type of training program to produce a new type of teacher. The faculty member must be willing to work on a team and share his strengths in an interdisciplinary atmosphere. Perhaps the most critical shift required will be in the faculty member's self-image: i.e., in terms of the program, he may have to change his self-image from "mathematics educator," for example, to "counselor of students," "evaluator of student performance," "research and development specialist," or "inschool, inservice support person." It seems clear that the problems of materials, devices, and facilities will be solved if the human resources are available and committed to the implementation of the plan.

Consequences

It is the authors' firm belief that the implementation of instructional technology in the teacher education curriculum will have a profoundly positive effect on the total field of education. We base this belief on the evidence already available from applications of both the the process and products of technology in research and development efforts throughout the United States. New models for teacher education will provide a vehicle for conducting longitudinal research that begins with the trainee's entrance into the program and continues to assess his teaching effectiveness throughout his career. This empirical orientation will provide teacher education with data indicating its effectiveness, and it should satisfy the increasing demands for accountability.

Of equal importance is the ability of educational technology to implement personalized and individualized instructional programs. The teacher trainee in such programs will be provided with a statement of desired learning outcomes, a series of empirically developed instructional materials, and performance oriented assessment. Faculty members will participate with students to help them achieve their objectives.

Applying technology to the education of teachers will have long-term, far-reaching effects. If these teachers teach as they were taught, the total impact of the technological curriculum will ultimately be felt at all levels of our schools.

8

Management Technology for Teacher Education

Position

If competency based teacher education programs are to be effective in realizing their objectives, it is essential that modern systems technology be employed in their management. Overall management is the business of planning, administering, and supervising all the activities of an ongoing instructional program and of providing resources such as facilities, personnel, and materials to keep the program in operation. It facilitates the total program by coordinating efforts, providing controls, and determining the quantity and quality of the program's products.

Rationale

As teacher education turns toward competency based programs and assumes accountability to a rapidly changing society, its processes will become increasingly complex. There will be a continuous and rapid input of new knowledge, innovative learning materials, improved techniques, and more effective equipment. Individualized instruction, which provides custom-made study programs, and changes in the nature of on-the-job training and other field experiences will require extensive scheduling systems. In addition, increased attention to program evaluation will require the collection, sorting, and frequent retrieval of vast amounts of data. To accomplish these management tasks and many others that are similarly complex, teacher educators must employ more effective approaches to management than those currently being used. The solution lies in the application of modern management technology.

Modern management technology is a system of ideas, principles, and techniques designed to help man reach his goals, provide the products he desires, solve technical problems, develop programs and strategies, and maintain complex operations. It is a product of man's creativity, designed to serve man and be controlled by him. Society has become increasingly dependent on it in recent years. It is used to manage military operations, industrial production, and space explorations. It is also effective in the management of government, communication systems, and public transportation.

Contrary to the opinions of some, technology does not necessarily imply the use of expensive hardware such as computers. Rather, the ideas, principles, and techniques of technology determine what hardware is needed, if any, and how, when, and where it should be used.

The basic concept underlying this approach to management is the validity of a systematic procedure in dealing with planning operations. We must begin by clearly understanding our objectives, make detailed plans to achieve these objectives, and then put our plans into effect while constantly evaluating and improving our methods. This basic notion has been extended into a system of complex interrelated principles of management. At the risk of oversimplification, the author has expressed some of the more significant principles in relatively nontechnical language to illustrate their applicability to the management of teacher education programs.

1. Define the mission and state its objectives.

2. Participants in a project must realize that the product—whether an idea, an object, a person, or a system—can and will be continually subjected to processing for improvement.

3. Whatever the plan or strategy, it must be regarded as flexible. Although there must be a detailed, logical, and efficient plan for operation, workers must constantly review and revise this plan, reallocating time and resources as necessary.

4. Each task within an activity must be clearly defined in order to manage appropriate skills and knowledge most efficiently.

5. A continuous search must be made for all relevant information that could affect the nature of the operation or the product. This information must be fed into the system at designated points.

Conditions Necessary for Implementation

A Basic Implication

A basic implication of the position taken in this chapter is that the management staff must understand systems technology; they must know how to apply its principles and use its techniques. In-service training programs must be designed to further the staff's understanding of the principles of systems technology and teach the skills necessary for application of its devices and techniques.

One of the devices of modern management technology is the Program Evaluation Review Technique (PERT). This is a valuable tool for depicting the network of events that must take place if a predicted outcome is to be achieved. This graphic model of the plan is accompanied by a time line, and for each activity there is a list of required resources, such as personnel, materials, and facilities. A proposed list of necessary resources is prepared from the information contained in the lists accompanying the PERT diagram. PERT diagrams are used for both short-term and long-term planning. They can be either simple or complex. Figure 1 illustrates a segment of a highly sophisticated PERT chart diagram. It depicts the flow of events for one phase of a multimillion dollar proposed educational program development project.

Another essential device of modern management technology is the flow chart. This is used to reveal the interrelationships among factors of concern, trace the flow of information among sources, and provide models of the flow of activities and events within systems. Figure 2 is a flow chart of a hypothetical student's movement through a series of experiences designed to provide him with particular teaching competencies.

Implications for the Concerns of Management

There is no attempt made here to discuss all implications of applying systems to management's concerns. By way of illustration we shall discuss some of the most conspicuous of management's concerns, including personnel selection, program operation, budgeting, scheduling, and providing for humanization.

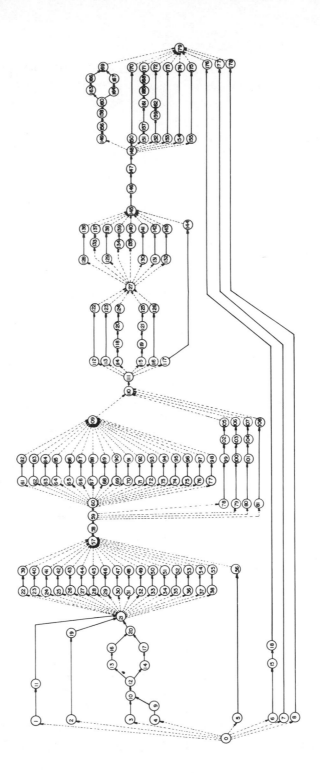

Fig. 1. Conceptual network for development of professional phase of model program

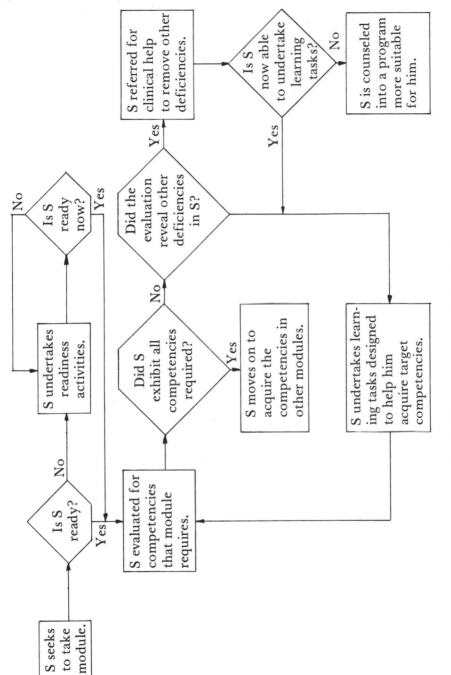

Fig. 2. Flow chart for individualized learning processes

Personnel Selection

The persons who will carry out the program must either have the essential job skills before they are employed or be capable of acquiring them. This implication is particularly important, because competency based teacher education programs require a variety of jobs and skills not characteristic of traditional programs. Operationally, this means that overall management must define each position in the program in relation to the specific activities to be performed and prepare job descriptions. The following is an illustration of a job description for an assistant director for student evaluation.

EVALUATION TECHNICAL ASSISTANT

Nature of Work

Teams who develop modular learning materials for teacher education programs require technical assistance in designing and piloting new evaluation procedures and devices. This is particularly true in new individualized competency based teacher education programs where emphasis is placed on assessing cognitive, psychomotor, and affective performance. The evaluation technical assistant works under the supervision of the director of the evaluation subsystem. He assists the materials development teams in designing proposed procedures and devices to determine the extent to which students have acquired the competencies associated with the modules and monitors the piloting and application of the proposed procedures and devices.

Illustrative Examples of Work

During planning and designing conferences serves as technical consultant to materials development teams regarding procedures and devices for evaluation.

Reviews all proposed evaluation procedures and devices with higher level evaluation specialists. Edits or revises as instructed.

Observes and reports validity and reliability information on all newly developed procedures and/or devices. Makes periodic checks of established evaluation devices with a view toward revision where necessary.

Desirable Knowledge, Abilities, and Skills

A sound understanding of the theoretical and operational principles affecting an individualized competency based teacher education program.

The ability to work cooperatively with others in specialties other than his who do not have special knowledge in his field.

A broad understanding of the theory and practice of modern approaches to evaluation (as distinguished from traditional tests and measurement) and skill in the application of them.

Knowledge of available standard tests, examinations, checklists, and other such devices and materials that may be applicable in teacher education programs.

Skill in writing, revising, and editing behavioral objectives.

Skill in preparing test items, making item analyses, and preparing reports for statistical analyses performed on evaluation procedures and devices.

Performs related work as required.

Desirable Training and Experience

Competency in evaluation, tests and measurement, statistics, educational psychology, curriculum, and guidance. Experience in an individualized educational program based on behavioral objectives, performance criteria, or competencies.

Management must continually survey existing personnel resources and determine when present personnel must be retrained to perform new tasks. As new positions are defined for which there are no available personnel, a search must be made for persons to fill them. For example, teacher education programs using modern management technology will require an increasing number of educational programs systems analysts, computer programmers, media specialists, systems technicians, counselors, and accountants. In addition, overall management must provide a suitable continuous inservice training program to handle specific personnel needs as assignments change and new personnel are brought into the program.

Program Operation

The management of competency based teacher education programs must be characterized by flexibility. The design of the program or any of its subsystems or components will always be subject to change. Modern management technology assumes a constantly changing environment for any system and requires that management activities be designed to accommodate this change. This is accomplished through a dynamic process of program operation, feedback, and revision.

Effective program operation requires continuous evaluation of the overall effectiveness of the instructional program in relation to its objectives. The purpose of continuous evaluation is to find new and better ways of providing appropriately prepared teachers for changing conditions. In evaluation each activity is assessed in relation to the overall purpose of the combined activities. The assessment includes such questions as: To what extent are the various activities producing the desired effects on student behaviors? How can the activities be improved? Once students become teachers, do the competencies they have acquired through the program actually help them to be effective teachers? Is overall management providing learning materials and facilities efficiently? Are there more efficient ways to accomplish any of the objectives and still maintain the desired quality?

The data obtained from this process is used to make decisions on modifications in the program, thus producing systematic revision. Programs characterized by this dynamic process of operation, evaluation, feedback, and revision are called *regenerative,* because they continue to grow, adapt, and improve in relation to the objectives of the program.

Program Budgeting

It has been traditional in teacher education to prepare budgets covering one-year periods and to allocate funds by items or departments. Allocations are often made according to some principle of fair distribution, such as numbers of students enrolled in classes. Such a plan tends to maintain the traditional organization, leaving little room for innovation or change.

Overall management must have a budgeting system that provides for change and innovation. Modern management technology facilitates such an approach by its endorsement of Planning, Programing and Budgeting Systems (PPBS). The assumption underlying PPBS is that a budget should represent a long-term set of plans designed to accomplish a particular mission. PPBS is characterized by flexibility; funds can be reallocated as frequently as program needs require. Planning, programing, and budgeting are seen as interrelated processes to be dealt with collectively, and they are subject to continuous evaluation.

The principles of PPBS require consideration of such questions as: How have changing conditions affected the mission? What intermediary objectives have been accomplished? What objectives have yet to be accomplished? Was the original allocation of resources sufficient? Was the anticipated progress made during the current period? What reallocation or redistribution of resources is necessary at this point? The results of the assessment determine budget adjustments. Such an approach to budgeting not only provides adaptability to change and new opportunities, but also tends to put all workers on the same team. The common mission reaches across departments and causes individuals as well as departments to reexamine the importance of their activities in relation to the mission.

Scheduling

The overall management of the new teacher education programs must carry out scheduling programs that combine students, instructors, facilities, materials, and equipment in sufficient numbers and kinds at the appropriate time in the student's instructional pattern. The computer programs currently in use in most universities and colleges simply assist in assigning students and their professors to classrooms, seminars, field experiences, and laboratories. Since competency based teacher education assumes that each student differs from all others in his specific educational needs, this approach to scheduling will soon be inadequate.

Providing Humanization

In today's educational world, the individual seems to have all but lost his identity. Today a college student is not far wrong if he believes that most persons with whom he associates on campus see him primarily as an "ID" number on the records. Campuses and classes are often so large that a student is in the presence of hundreds of people a day but knows few of them well because the pace of his life is so rapid.

Management systems presently used for higher education appear to have left humanization to chance. Perhaps it was not necessary to plan humanization when communities and societies were smaller and relatively stable and the pace of life was less rapid. We can no longer afford this neglect. Management must use the techniques of modern technology to provide occasions for human interaction that will help students realize and maintain their own identity and respect the identities of others.

9

Multi-Institutional Organization Patterns in Teacher Education

Wilford A. Weber

Position

We are committed to teacher education organizational patterns that are multi-institutional in nature. Operationally, this means that responsibility for the education of teachers should be shared by colleges, schools, and the educational community broadly defined.

Rationale

Under the usual organizational pattern of teacher education programs the teacher education institution—a college or university— has the major, if not the sole responsibility for the preservice education of teachers. That responsibility has been shared to some extent with schools, but only with regard to the student teaching experience. The extent of this cooperation has been largely limited to the school's providing a setting in which the student teacher practices teaching under the guidance of a master teacher. Control, however, has remained largely in the hands of the college. In future teacher education programs colleges should share much more of their responsibility with schools and other segments of the educational community.

Such multi-institutional patterns will undoubtedly take many different forms. However, it seems that the groups sharing teacher education responsibilities will at least include colleges, schools, government educational agencies, and educational industries. In addition, educational professional organizations, state departments of education, college students and student organizations, members of the community and the "noneducation" academic disciplines will be more involved in teacher education programs than at present.

The movement toward multi-institutional organizations and the greater involvement of "peripheral" elements are means of achieving two important objectives: (1) to maximize the resources available to teacher education programs, and (2) to involve more closely those both directly and indirectly concerned in the decision-making processes related to teacher education. This chapter examines the contributions multi-institutional organizations can make to the achievement of those two objectives. More specifically, this chapter briefly describes the nature and extent of the possible contributions of each of the various segments of the educational community: colleges, schools, government educational agencies, educational industries, educational professional organizations, teacher education students, the community, and noneducation disciplines.

Conditions Necessary for Implementation

The College and the Consortium

Traditionally, the college's major function has been to provide a setting where the student can experience instruction to facilitate his acquisition of specified teaching competencies. Operationally, this means that the college has provided the personnel, materials, and facilities constituting the bulk of the instructional program. Another important, but often overlooked, contribution of the college is the conduct of educational research. While this characterization is somewhat oversimplified, it does describe the traditional functions of the college in the teacher education program.

Whatever one's feelings about the present effectiveness of colleges in the education of teachers, they clearly have valuable resources—personnel, materials, and facilities—to contribute to the process. Therefore, a pattern of organization that fails to recognize the college's assets denies itself potentially valuable resources. Since our colleges presently face considerable financial difficulties, it seems reasonable to suggest that recognition of their resources should include consideration of the benefits to be derived from consortia arrangements.

Consortia of colleges take many forms, but their common element is the establishment of mutually beneficial working relationships among a number of colleges. These relationships may be formal or informal, short-term or long-term, task specific or more general in nature. The preference here is for relatively formal, long-term relationships that focus specifically on both preservice and inservice education of teachers.

Faculty members are perhaps the greatest resource of a college. By bringing together a number of colleges and their faculties, a consortium increases the number of faculty members available to undertake a particular task or set of tasks relevant to the teacher education program. In this respect, then, the consortium concept is built on the "two heads are better than one" principle.

A consortium also expands the instructional facilities and materials available to the college and the student. This is particularly important, because teacher education programs are placing increasing emphasis on the use of media and hardware. Cooperative materials production and computer time sharing are only two examples of the advantages a consortium arrangement might offer.

There are many examples of successful teacher education consortia. The Consortium of Southern Colleges for Teacher Education, National Center for Educational Research and Development, is in the process of designing teacher education program based on the principles of the Elementary Teacher Education Program Models. The Cooperative Urban Teacher Education Program, an effective program for educating teachers for the inner city, is a cooperative venture of nearly twenty colleges, two public school systems, a regional council for higher education, and a regional laboratory in the Kansas City area. The College Center of thee Finger Lakes in upstate New York is a consortium of ten colleges. And perhaps one of the best examples of a consortium in light of this discussion is the Consortium of the Universities of Ohio, which was responsible for the design of one of the Elementary Teacher Education Program Models. The organizational structure of each of these examples is quite different, but all have in common the sharing of resources through institutional cooperation.

Clearly, the major benefits of a consortium of colleges are the expansion of resources and the sharing of ideas. It is equally clear, however, that participating colleges must overcome problems of identity, trust, and communication if they are to receive the full benefit of this pattern of organization. This seems to be a reasonably small risk considering the potential gains. Achieving an organization that maximizes the resources available to each participating institution is not an easy task. The benefits to be derived, however, seem to warrant the effort; the alternative—a "go-it-alone" pattern or organization—seems far less attractive.

The Schools

The emphasis that competency based teacher education places on field experience mandates close cooperation between the college and schools, because competency based programs require continuous reality testing of program outputs and the schools provide the best situation for such testing. The schools not only furnish settings in which teacher education students confront real pupils but also provide skilled personnel to guide the student. School personnel will become integral parts of the differentiated staffing patterns that increasingly characterize teacher education programs and, consequently, will become part of the decision-making structure.

A strong case supporting this viewpoint was made in a recent publication of the American Association of Colleges for Teacher Education.

> Closer school and college relationships are imperative. New mechanisms and new structures are being formed. These new structures call for new roles and fundamental rearrangements of responsibilities. Schools are finding their way toward including teacher education as primary, high-priority function. Customary arrangements for student teaching are being remodeled here and there . . . for change to become progress, the ferment in teacher education needs full cooperation of schools and colleges and a fundamental review of purposes, functions, and roles and responsibilities.
>
> The clinical experience in teacher education can be enormously strengthened through collaboration between universities and schools with support from state agencies and professional organizations. . . . A clinical approach to teaching should be a priority element in the continuing education of teachers, as well as in pre-service programs of student teaching and internship. The instructional goal for cooperative enterprise in teacher education might be stated as follows: To facilitate the realistic study of teaching in relation to theoretical propositions about teaching.[1]

At first glance, the type of cooperation described above may appear to be the present condition, and in some ways it is. However, many things will be quite different in the future, including (1) the amount of time the college student will spend in the schools, and (2) the role of school personnel in teacher education.

Clearly, students will be spending far more of their time interacting with children and teachers in the schools; teaching experiences will occur earlier and more frequently in the student's preparation and will last for longer periods. The semester of student teaching at the end of the senior year will be a thing of the past. The student's on-the-job training may begin in his freshman year with "early awareness" experiences; continue through one-to-one tutoring, small group teaching, and total class responsibilities; and culminate in fifth-year resident internships.

The very close school-college working relationship prescribed by the Teacher Corps guidelines in an example of a pattern that will become more common as its effectiveness is demonstrated.[2] The Elementary Teacher Education Program Models have also placed great value on the cooperation of colleges and schools. The following brief statements from the Ohio Consortium, Michigan State University, and Florida State University models are typical:

> Another assumption relative to the basic approach to training teachers is that there will be considerable involvement of the public schools as the physical facility for a substantial part of the training. The specifications cannot be operationally implemented by a university or college with no public (or private) elementary school involvement. The assumption is that public schools and universities can put forth a cooperative and coordinated effort. To some extent this approach would parallel present cooperation between medical schools and selected hospitals in the training of medical doctors.[3]

> Within the state or region served by the implementing institution, local school agencies (school districts) must be identified and articulated with the teacher education program.[4]

> All of this adds up to the logical conclusion that the pre-service—in-service phases are part of a continuum, and that to varying degrees, schools, universities, and state departments of education will need to be involved at each step along the way.[5]

Indeed, the Michigan State University Model goes on to explain its "clinical-school network" concept (a training and research complex); the University of Wisconsin model speaks of the "school network" approach; and the Florida State University model describes its "portal school" notion, a means of facilitating entry into the profession. The point is clear: new and closer relationships between colleges and schools will characterize teacher education programs of the future.

School personnel will play a much more active role in the decision-making processes of the teacher education program. They will be involved in specifying objectives and competencies, designing instructional activities, evaluating student and program progress, and making policy. In short, the school will become an equal partner with the college in the preparation of teachers. Indeed, several school people have suggested that unless they are treated as peers by college personnel, schools may completely withdraw from teacher education. If competency based teacher education is to be effective, the nature of school-college relationships will need to change dramatically. The benefits to be gained from healthy relationships are many; the consequences of poor relationships are likely to be detrimental; and the complete lack of relationships could prove disastrous.

Government Educational Agencies

Teacher education of the future will find greater cooperation between colleges and federal and state programs concerned with teacher education such as Teacher Corps, Training the Trainers of Teachers projects, protocol materials projects, Model Cities programs, regional educational research centers, and Title III supplementary centers. A much closer working relationship will be established between colleges and such agencies as agency outputs are employed in teacher education programs. In short, the products of educational governmental agencies, which remain largely theoretical, will become more meaningful as colleges use and evaluate them. The closer the relationships between such agencies and colleges, the more profitable their experience. The mutual benefits derived from these relationships will make such patterns of organization increasingly attractive.

Perhaps the clearest example of a government agency in this type of role, is the Northwest Regional Educational Laboratory which was the main designer of the Elementary Teacher Education Program Models. Another example is the Far West Regional Laboratory, which has contributed through the development of its "mini-courses." The Eastern Regional Institute for Education, which joined two Title III centers in a feasibility study of the Syracuse University Protocooperative model, is yet another example.

Clearly, if the products of the various government educational projects and agencies are to be useful, their activities must be more closely articulated with the activities of teacher education institutions. Direct involvement of government educational agencies—on a peer basis—in the design, development, and opeation of teacher education programs seems the best response to this need for articulation.

Educational Industries

Future teacher education programs will cooperate more fully with educational industries. The publishers of instructional materials and educational consulting firms will become members of the teacher education "team" and will see themselves as having teacher education responsibilities although they are not teacher educators per se.

Much of the necessary instructional material for competency based teacher education programs does not presently exist. It needs to be produced, and it makes sense to put that production in the hands not only of those who have designed the program and have the substantive understandings required, but also of those who have the required technical competence. This suggests increased collaboration between college personnel and publishers of educational materials. Recent decisions regarding copyright policies make such collaboration even more attractive to educational publishers.

The complexity of competency based teacher education programs makes inputs from educational consultants with particular technological and managerial skills quite valuable. For example, the systems approach, which it is hoped will characterize teacher education programs, requires managerial and planning competencies not usually found among teacher educators. Certain consultants from the educational industry do have these competencies. Close working relationships between industry and program will allow those competencies to be tapped.

The effective involvement of a representative educational industry in the conduct of nearly all the Elementary Teacher Education Program Models feasibility studies is rather meaningful evidence in support of this viewpoint. The recent copyrighted publication of certain of the Far West Regional Educational Laboratory mini-courses by a commercial publishing firm is quite possibly a prelude to the kinds of cooperative efforts we can come to expect. Further, while it is not concerned with higher education and the preparation of teachers, the Texarkana Performance Contract Experiment may be a preview of educational industry participation of an even more radical kind. The type and degree of the educational industry's involvement in teacher education programs is still undefined. However, it is clear that a new type of interaction is emerging, and that interaction is more intimate than in the past.

Educational Professional Organizations

In the future the educational professional organizations will play a more active role in teacher education. While these organizations will probably not become part of the teacher education organizational pattern, their personnel will be consulted more frequently. It is entirely possible that they will have representatives on the policy-making boards of teacher education institutions; indeed, such representation seems highly desirable.

David Darland makes a particularly strong argument for the intimate involvement of professional organizations in teacher education in *Teachers for the Real World.*[6] He suggests that the teaching profession should have certain powers, including licensure and certification of teachers, accreditation of teacher education institutions, and development of programs, studies, and research designed to improve teacher education.[7] While these prescriptions may come to pass, the prediction here is that these responsibilities will remain largely in the hands of state departments of education, who will continue to share aspects of them with other institutions and agencies.

The importance of the inputs professional organizations can make is fairly obvious. Of equal importance, however, is the two-way communication produced by a healthy working relationship. There are obvious advantages to giving the professional organizations a platform from which to voice their opinions and an opportunity to be involved in decisions that will ultimately influence the profession. Increasing teacher militancy requires particularly intelligent consideration of the role professional organizations are to play in teacher education. The prediction here is that the contributions of professionals will be valued and, therefore, welcomed. The alternative is an unproductive struggle for power.

State Departments of Education

The roles played by state departments of education in teacher education programs vary greatly from state to state. Involvement now ranges from funding experimental programs and encouraging innovation to simply certifying teachers and perpetuating the status quo. Teacher education programs of the future will directly involve personnel from state departments of education. Such persons will be an influential part of the decision-making process at each stage of development and operation. Most importantly they will be called on to help resolve the many problems having to do with certification of competency based program graduates: a difficult issue already being attacked by state departments of education in Florida, New York, Texas, and Washington. Perhaps this viewpoint is best summarized by the statement, quoted earlier from the Florida State University model, that "state departments of education will need to be involved [in the teacher education program] at each step along the way."[8]

Teacher Education Students

Teacher education of the future will be much more "consumer oriented" than is presently the case. The topics of personalization, individualization, and humanization have been explored elsewhere in this volume, and there is no need to repeat those discussions here. However, it is important to note that future teacher education programs will give students opportunities for making decisions about both their own educational programs and the total program. In other words, students will have a hand in the policy-making processes at each stage of the program's development and operation.

Recent events on our college campuses strongly suggest the need to involve students in shaping their education. Indeed, the benefits of such involvement are clear. First among these is the depolarization achieved through the trust and open communication that can develop from honest and amicable interaction between students and faculty. What better learning experience can there be than involvement in and responsibility for one's own learning program? In light of the present mood, there appears to be no sensible alternative.

The Community

Future teacher education programs will have increased contact with the community. On one hand, students will be given an opportunity to examine the school within the community context; on the other hand, members of the community will be given opportunities to make contributions to the program. A field oriented curriculum will encourage the former; differentiated staffing and community representation in the decision-making structure will encourage the latter. It seems a bit strange that most parents are presently unable to influence either the education of the students working with their children or the nature of the student-child interaction. Although community influence would probably be exerted on teacher education programs in informal ways, the channels for community inputs should be kept open.

At present, community involvement in the teacher education program and student involvement in the community is perhaps best exemplified in Teacher Corps programs. Interns are expected to participate fully in the life of the community in which they are teaching, and community representatives are encouraged to participate in the planning and operation of the instructional program. This is the kind of relationship that teacher education programs of the future will have with the community.

Noneducation Disciplines

The future teacher education program will do a far better job of putting its own house in order. Communication with disciplines other than education per se will be improved; the curriculum will be more integrated; the nature of the interaction between liberal arts and professional programs will change; a wider range of electives will be offered; and there will be greater opportunities for interdisciplinary offerings. In short, teacher education will become an institution-wide function unfettered by the artificial boundaries now so common in institutions of higher education.

While all of the Elementary Teacher Education Model Programs emphasize the need to develop strong working relationships between teacher educators and those in other colleges within the university, the University of Massachusetts model makes a particularly strong case for interdisciplinary approaches to teacher education: "As a general proposition, we believe that the success of any teacher-training program relevant for our times depends on better cooperation and interaction between a school of education and other schools in the university."[9] Silberman makes a similar plea in *Crisis in the Classroom:*

> The remaking of American education thus requires a new kind of relationship within the university between the faculties of education and the faculties of arts and sciences, law, medicine, journalism, social work, and so on, as well as new kinds of relationships between universities and public schools.[10]

To take a different position seems foolhardy, for it denies the student access to resources that can help him become both a more effective generalist and a more competent specialist. The move toward differentiated staffing patterns makes the inputs of non-education disciplines crucial to the preparation of teachers.

The Protocooperative

Perhaps this chapter gives the impression that the teacher education program of the future will be like the hub of a wheel with various institutions within the educational community linked to it like spokes. This is not the organizational pattern envisioned for future teacher education programs. Instead, teacher education programs will include all the elements discussed above in the kind of partnership arrangement that some have called protocooperatives.

Perhaps the feasibility report of the Syracuse University model program best describes this concept of protocooperation:

> We assume that the preparation of teachers should be increasingly a joint endeavor involving a variety of professional and lay groups. For example, we assume that such institutions as universities, public schools, industries, regional educational agencies, student groups, parent and lay public groups should be in some way involved in the planning, implementation, and on-going evaluation of teacher education programs.
>
> We assume that the Model Program . . . . will operate most effectively in the context of protocooperation. (Protocooperation refers to a condition in which two or more organisms in interaction mutually benefit from non-obligatory relationships. When the organisms are not in interaction, no harm accrues to any of the organisms. In this case, organisms refer to both institutions and people.) We assume the continued existence and interaction of a variety of groups and agencies concerned with the education of teachers. We further assume that the optimum functioning of this Model Program is ultimately dependent upon the quality of interaction implied by the concept of protocooperation. We recognize that protocooperation . . . . is not a precondition for implementation. It is an ideal toward which adopters of this Model should strive.[11]

Footnotes

1. B. Othanel Smith, *Teachers for the Real World* (Washington, D.C.: American Assoc. of Colleges for Teacher Education, 1967).

2. *Teacher Corps Guidelines for 1971-1973* (Washington, D.C.: U.S. Office of Education, 1970), pp. 3-7.

3. University of Toledo, *Educational Specifications for a Comprehensive Elementary Teacher Education Program,* vol. 1 (Washington, D.C.: Government Printing Office, 1969), p. 129.

4. Michigan State University, *Behavioral Science Teacher Education Program,* vol. 3 (Washington, D.C.: Government Printing Office, 1969), p. 169.

5. Florida State University, *A Model for the Preparation of Elementary School Teachers,* vol. 1 (Washington, D.C.: Government Printing Office, 1969), pp. 15-23.

6. David Darland, "Preparation in the Governance of the Profession," in *Teachers for the Real World,* ed. B. Othanel Smith(Washington, D.C.: American Assoc. of Colleges for Teacher Education, 1969), pp. 135-49.

7. Ibid., p. 142.

8. Florida State University, *A Model,* p. 117.

9. University of Massachusetts, *Model Elementary Teacher Education Program* (Washington, D.C.: Government Printing Office, 1969), p. 50.

10. Charles E. Silberman, *Crisis in the Classroom* (New York: Random House, 1970), p. 517.

11. Syracuse University Protocooperative, *A Study of the Feasibility of the Refined Syracuse University Specifications for a Comprehensive Undergraduate and Inservice Teacher Education Program for Elementary Teachers* (Washington, D.C.: Government Printing Office, 1970), pp. 13-14.

10
Changing Teacher Education Faculty Roles

William Wiersma, Jr.

George E. Dickson

Position

Even a cursory examination of recent developments in teacher education reveals the inadequacy of present university faculty roles for meeting the needs of teacher education. Traditionally the university faculty member has been relatively isolated from external forces and resistant to change. Teacher education faculties share this isolation and resistance to change. Teacher education has been grounded in local and regional traditions. It has not been subjected to systematic evaluation nor based on organized empirical research. Attempts at improvement have been fragmentary with limited directions and only short-range goals. Present demands for change come from a variety of sources, both inside and outside the profession, and have rendered existing practices intolerable. Our basic position is that there will be a marked change in teacher education faculty roles and that this change will be induced with relative speed.

Rationale

Present teacher education programs are much as they were at the close of World War II. The general course of study includes general education of a broad nature stressing Western cultural concerns, the usual professional courses (child development, methods, curriculum), field experiences, and possibly some opportunity for limited subject matter specialization. The resulting teacher education program is incongruous in modern technological society, is irrelevant to basic social issues, and discourages creativity in professionals preparing to teach at all levels in our schools. Unfortunately, young teachers who go into the schools for a lifetime career from these limited and conservative teacher education bases can depend on only an occasional inservice education activity to update their understanding, skills and appreciation. Documentation of these general theses in educational literature has been frequent and voluminous.[1] It needs no repeating here. What is needed is an understanding that changes in teacher education faculty roles will require substantial efforts to counter the inertia that characterizes present teacher education.

The crux of this task is the teacher's preparation for the classroom. Preparation programs must be designed to create teachers who see themselves as change agents whose job is both to create change and to function effectively in a constantly changing environment. That changing environment can be viewed at both micro and macro levels. At the micro level, teachers in the classroom need to improve their understanding that each year children come to them from a different society from the one that children came from the year before. Society is changing, and those changes are reflected in the attitudes, thoughts, and needs of children. To respond sensitively to these children requires a practical recognition and awareness of the child's changing world.

At the macro level, teachers need to recognize that the nature of their profession and their careers changes perceptibly from year to year and dramatically from one decade to the next. Many of today's graduates of teacher preparation institutions will retire early in the twenty-first century. As the nature of our society changes, so will the schools, and so must the roles teachers assume in those schools. It is already late. Schools and teachers everywhere serve outmoded functions. While we must prepare teachers for more effective roles in today's schools, we must also help them project their perceptions to the future with the realistic goal of increasing effectiveness as teachers by continuing to reflect the nature of the society they serve.

Conditions Necessary for Implementation

This chapter focuses less on new roles than on changing roles.

To focus development effort on the creation of new roles is merely to create a new role for a new structure, both of which could be expected to reach obsolescence at a very early date. The need is for a better understanding of all that is involved in evolving or changing faculty roles. This task is difficult in the schools and nearly impossible in the colleges and universities, where academic freedom is highly valued and substantially maintained. If college or university faculties are to become committed to a teacher education that reflects the values and needs of a changing society, we must find ways of providing teacher education in contexts that are themselves constantly changing.

Specializing Teacher Education Faculty Roles

One characteristic of the future faculty role will be increasing specialization, which will take forms different from those of the present. We now have the curriculum specialist, the educational psychologist, the science specialist, and the like. These specialties are still rather broadly defined, and in most situations the teacher educator specialist is involved in many peripheral activities. Universities often have teacher education faculty playing many roles, not all of which are suited to their talents. These roles include teacher, supervisor, and counselor. The philosophy that "everybody should be doing everything" is no longer tenable, however; it is an inefficient approach, which at best tends to encourage mediocrity in several activities rather than excellence in one. The new roles will require excellence in the particular skills of the faculty member's specialty. Thus, greater faculty competence may be anticipated.

Specialties will change markedly from those of the present. Certainly some, such as subject area specialties, will be retained at least for a while, but others will be eliminated and new ones will take their place. All specialties will be viewed as dynamic rather than static, and no professor will ever reach the pinnacle of his speciality—in terms of "resting on his laurels"—during his professional career. There will be continuous pressure on faculty to revise their roles to reflect the needs of a changing school in a changing society.

Learning Specialists

There has been considerable discussion and controversy about learning theories, the teaching process, and the relationship between the two on both conceptual and operational levels. The increasing use of behavioral objectives, educational specifications, and evaluation of educational outcomes in teacher education has stimulated a review of various psychological positions. Now we must recognize the importance of this component in the process of developing and operating exemplary teacher education programs. There is a great deal of information about the learning-teaching process that is not being effectively used to provide direction in designing and implementing teacher education programs.

A behavioral approach to teacher education will put more emphasis on outcomes, behaviors, and the overt operational procedures and techniques that produce specific behaviors. There will be greater opportunity to develop and test ideas related to the learning-teaching process. The role of the learning specialist will not be separated, in theory or practice, from the real world of teaching. All this will enhance the learning specialist's role and increase its importance in teacher education processes.

Research and Evaluation Specialists

The statements and descriptions of new teacher education programs strongly imply that specialists will be trained for roles in developmental research and evaluation. The research will relate to the improvement of preservice and inservice training programs for elementary and secondary teachers and will be conducted within the context of an operating instructional system. This will require personnel trained in the new research methodology and competent to conduct research within the bounds of operating systems. The researcher will be a member of the team operating the system.

Much emphasis will be placed on empirical evaluation. The term *evaluation* implies an ongoing process that supports decision making. It involves continuous collection of information, monitoring of instructional and other systems, and effective feedback processes. This type of evaluation requires special competencies not commonly found in education at present. Evaluation and research specialists will have important roles in teacher education, and substantial portions of those roles will be noninstructional.

Educational Technology Specialists

The influence of technology on education will have a marked effect on teacher education faculties. It will require a group of specialists to instruct students in the uses of electronic media and to help other faculty members improve their effectiveness through the use of media. Technological hardware and software innovations will involve cooperation with business and industry. Educational industry will undoubtedly expand its role in teacher education, and personnel from industry may be expected to function as technology specialists on teacher education teams.

Instructional Specialists

Instruction in teacher education programs will shift from general information transmission to instructional guidance, demonstration, and modeling. To become an effective instructional guide and learning manager, the future teacher should experience these roles as a college learner. For example, there will be increasing emphasis on individualized instruction and personalized attention in our schools, but such education cannot be demonstrated in a classroom lecture to 400 students. Team teaching on the elementary school level is another accelerating trend. It will be necessary for teacher education faculty to demonstrate or model effectively the principles of team teaching.

What does it mean to specialize as a learning manager, model, or demonstrator? It means that certain specially trained faculty members are adept builders and organizers of learning activities. In this building and organizing process, these specialists will increasingly become learners along with their students. Learning will become more a cooperative activity and less a one-way communication from professor to student. Students will play an increasing role as partners in the learning process and thus will be increasingly involved in decision making, not only about themselves but also about the entire teacher education program. The future teacher will teach by demonstrating through his own behavior a commitment to the process of inquiry and learning. This must also be the model for the teacher educator, be he professor, public school teacher, specialist, or whatever.

Peripheral Roles

Technology

The teacher of teachers will increasingly be required to use the products of modern technology in his professional activities. This implies (1) using electronic media, computers, etc., in working with the teacher education program, and (2) preparing students to use technological products in their teaching careers. Both faculty and students must have positive attitudes toward modern technology and must develop appropriate skills for its use.

Teacher education programs must place greater emphasis on individualizing programs for students. Individualized programs require continuous assessment, monitoring, and feedback. With normal enrollments, this will be physically impossible without an organized information collection and processing system and assistance from electronic equipment. But the system and the equipment will be useless unless the professor understands his role as an integral part of the system. Professors are not to become computer operators, but they must be proficient in data management, organization, and interpretation. Considerable amounts of information will be at their disposal, and if effective decisions for individualized instruction are to be made, the information will have to be used effectively and efficiently.

The future teacher's use of modern technology products can best be modeled by the cooperative efforts of one or more technology specialists and other members of the teacher education team. This will also require new skills on the part of the teacher education professor, but these should be compatible with and supportive of his own use of technology.

Support Personnel

Aside from the hardware and software of technology, the teacher education professor will increasingly receive assistance from support personnel. Increased and continuous monitoring of the instructional process is one activity that will require support personnel. Certainly the faculty member will be involved in such activities, and increased cooperation with support personnel will be a necessary characteristic of his role. The various functions of team members and support personnel will need to be identified and described for specific situations. Such description is a matter reserved for more detailed consideration, but the point remains that this type of cooperative effort will affect the faculty member's role.

Systems Management

Exemplary programs of teacher education will involve management and control systems of varying degrees of complexity.[2] Some will be relatively extensive, consisting of several subsystems. Continuous data collection, monitoring, and feedback are common characteristics of such systems. It is certainly to be expected that program adjustments, corrections, and revisions will be commonplace and will be based on continuously updated data. (The management control system of the program should not be confused with data collection and monitoring of student progress. Although the latter would undoubtedly be a part of the former, the control system of the program would involve other factors such as budgeting and scheduling.)

What influence will the inclusion of a management and control system have on the role of the teacher education professor? Will the system serve as a mechanical watchdog? Will the computer being used for data analysis be viewed in the same way that some taxpayers view the equipment that processes their annual returns? It is hoped that neither will be the case. However, an efficient management and control system will introduce factors of accountability not now common in higher education instruction. The faculty member will find himself making more interim decisions that adjust the program to meet desired outcomes. In order to make better decisions the professor will need to become proficient in the manipulation, coordination, and interpretation of information, especially empirical data. The future role of the teacher education professor will involve increased decision making subject to assessment in terms of program effectiveness.

Research

This discussion may imply that the professor's role will center entirely on program operation to the exclusion of research and teaching. This is not at all the case. Just as the function of teaching will take on different characteristics, the function of research will now take on a new and more important character. As the opportunity for research, especially development research, increases, so will the need for such research. The opportunity and need for research, however, will add to the responsibilities of the teacher education faculty member, primarily in the area of empirical data production. Teacher education faculty will not be exclusively a group of research specialists. However, all members of the faculty will be required to be much more knowledgeable about elementary research procedures and principles than has been the case. In addition, their ability to apply these

principles will be subject to continuous evaluation. Research procedures must be regarded as useful tools for the professor's use, rather
than mysterious skills possessed by a small select group of the
faculty.

Accountability

A final point can be made relating to future accountability and
its effect on the professor's role. Several of the Office of Education's
elementary models contain systems for extensive assessment and
feedback on the placement and performance of their graduates. Such
systems will be much more empirical and organized than present
informal feedback from the field, and they will be another source of
information for program adjustment and change. Since public accountability will make it much more difficult to persist with an
inadequate program than it is now, the faculty member must learn to
use every available source of information and feedback to evaluate
and improve the program. However, the information will be used in
cooperation with other teacher education personnel, including those
off campus. Thus, education professors must learn to share with
other personnel an increasing responsibility for program decisions
and continued program development. This implies a new dimension
of accountability in the professor's role and a new responsibility-
accountability cycle.

Interinstitutional Cooperation

A dominant aspect of new teacher education programs is the
interinstitutional operation essential to the teacher education
process. Schools are presently used only for student teaching and
occasional internships, but new programs will involve a variety of
personnel outside traditional teacher education faculties. What effect
will this have on the role of the teacher educator? Perhaps the most
important effect will be that the university professor will have to
share his position as teacher educator. Because of the increasing emphasis on field and clinical experiences, school personnel who have
major responsibilities in the education of teachers will be appropriately recognized and will become functioning members of the team
on a new basis of parity.

The increasing influence of public school and other personnel is
partially due to the increasing emphasis in teacher education on the

effects of teacher behavior on the pupil. Some very hard direct questions are being asked about how teachers promote learning and what teachers do that makes a difference. Most of these questions are directly related to the focus on competency based certification and accountability programs. If the teacher education program is to be accountable in terms of product criteria based on pupil outcomes, it must cultivate a closer relationship with the schools.

In addition to schools, universities, and, potentially, the educational industry, there are other sources that will generate changes in the groups and persons serving in teacher education roles. Junior colleges and other collegiate institutions will function on reciprocal agreement bases. Regional educational laboratories and research and development centers will provide personnel for cooperative roles in teacher education. Even though many of these centers do not specifically claim a teacher education role, then programs have definite implications for teacher education.[3] Teacher educators cannot be oblivious to what is being done in these agencies; in order to use their results effectively, they must negotiate cooperative long-term arrangements and commitments. This is only a sampling of the new personnel and new relationships that will augment the lonely educator we find teaching in today's college of education.

Team Contexts

It is one thing to demand excellence and quite another to produce it. The future faculty role will have a team characteristic that will enhance both efforts to improve and chances of success. At present, most faculty members can pursue their professional activities in relative isolation if they wish. Moreover, the profession has many ways of protecting mediocre performance. Without adequate evaluation in the larger context, such performance is usually undetected by everyone, with the possible exception of some students. When the individual functions as a member of a professional team, however, the demand and even the motivation for excellence is much more acute. The team approach will become increasingly characteristic of the faculty role.

A word might be said at this point about the present development of faculty teams. Certainly there have been some attempts at team activities. But operationally this approach to program development and implementation is in its infancy. Probably the most productive teams to date have included only one professor and one or possibly several graduate students. The teacher education teams of the future will include several faculty members of varied status, and they will be on the team because of their fitness for the task to be done, not because of their status. Teams will also include professional personnel from other educational agencies and selected support personnel.

Administrative and Organizational Patterns

Turning our attention to existing departmental structures, we find that the exemplary model teacher education programs of the future imply quite different divisional structures. The Ohio Model, for example, categorized its educational specifications in five contexts: instructional organization, technology, social factors, contemporary learning-teaching processes, and research. All the models diminished the importance of the teacher's role as a transmitter of existing knowledge, and emphasized his role as a manager of learning. The implication is that teacher education faculties will be organized by process rather than by the traditional subject or professional areas. The divisions will follow a programed planning approach somewhat like that of the Department of Defense in the early 1960s. There, the traditional service divisions were replaced by such classifications as research and development. Recategorization and shifts in emphasis will require the demise of some old loyalties and the emergence of new identifications for the teacher education professor.

It is also appropriate to comment briefly on the changing role of the teacher education administrator. The administrator will not easily relinquish his decision-making role, but this role will change markedly in two ways: (1) it will become increasingly a facilitating leadership, i.e., a cooperative effort with faculty; and (2) with the inclusion of extensive management and control systems, it will become much more empirically organized, which will introduce a new dimension of accountability. As a result of these changes, the administrator will become only one of the many persons with whom a given professor shares responsibility for program decisions and management.

Consequences

What does all this mean in terms of changing roles for a teacher education faculty? Will the teacher educator be the maverick in his university setting? Will faculty roles in teacher education be so incompatible with faculty roles in other colleges that teacher education will be isolated in separate institutions? On the contrary, the new roles suggested for teachers of teachers are more compatible than ever with current university directions and developments in higher education. This implies that the solutions to many problems experienced by colleges and universities may require careful consideration of the concepts of faculty roles throughout the campus.

In his discussion of the changing college classroom, Lansky emphasizes the importance of individual differences and the ubiquitous nature of learning.[4] He also recognizes that shared responsibility for teaching and learning creates self-motivated learning in teachers and students. The idea that teacher education should include personnel from educational organizations outside the university and additional experiences off campus is supported by Wolff's concept of the multiversity. According to Wolff, "the multiversity, as its name suggests, exhibits none of the unity of place, purpose, and political organization which characterized older universities."[5] In the same article, Wolff emphasizes the value of technical knowledge. Additional references could be cited on the changing role and structure of the university, but those noted sufficiently support our belief that the position taken in this discussion has considerable consequences for the entire university community.

Technology and management systems will have a substantial influence on faculty roles. Many details must be explicated and value judgments considered, but there is conclusive evidence that the influence of technology on the educational process is here to stay and will increase. Thus, the influence of technology and systems on teacher education programs and their faculties is in keeping with what is occurring in education in general and in the university in particular.[6]

The teacher educator will become more a manager of instruction and less a transmitter of information. He will be part of an instructional team that will bring to teacher education new personnel with new skills. Team efforts and team membership will extend beyond the traditional sphere of activity of the university. The teacher educator will have support systems in both personnel and technology, and it will be his responsibility to use them effectively and efficiently. Evaluation, management, and adjustment of the program will be continuous functions of the faculty. Substantive decision making will be an increasingly real, continuing function of teacher education personnel.

The discussion throughout the chapter has been focused on the changing faculty role projected from recent developments in teacher education. Faculty has been defined broadly to include all who would teach teachers. The changing faculty role implies a major re-education of faculty, with all its content, procedure, and logistical detail. A host of issues has been raised in this context. It has not been our purpose to indicate all these issues or present suggestions for reeducation. That is left for another time and place. It is enough to say, in conclusion, that the faculty member will be the change agent in future teacher education process and progress. The faculty makes the real difference, and all design and development efforts, however extensive, require faculty understanding, direction, and support. American youth require dramatically different forms of education. These will be achieved only to the extent that faculty can change their concepts of their own roles in ways that provide both the direction and the force required to build the new school.

Footnotes

1. For example see, Committee for Economic Development, *Innovation in Education: New Directions for the American School* (New York: Committee for Economic Development, July 1968), pp. 14, 51; Kevin A. Ryan, "A Plan for a New Type of Professional Training for a New Type of Teaching Staff," *The Teacher and His Staff*, Occasional Papers, no. 2 (Washington, D.C.: NCTEPS, Nat'l Education Assoc., February 1968), p. 1; Edgar Dale, "New Media: Men and Machines," *The News Letter* 33 (May 1968): 4; Don Davies, "Practical and Potential Possibilities of EPDA and other USOE Supported Programs," in American Assoc. of Colleges for Teacher Education, *Teacher Education: Action for Americans* (Report of the 14th Biennial School for Executives, Washington, D.C., 1969), pp. 8–14.

2. For summary statements of these systems see Walt LeBaron, "Analytic Summaries of Specifications for Model Teacher Education Programs (Washington, D.C.: Nat'l Center for Educational Research and Development, Government Printing Office, 1970).

3. As examples we have the development of the multi-unit school concept by the Wisconsin Research and Development Center for Cognitive Learning and the extensive work in individually prescribed instruction done by the Pittsburgh Research and Development Center.

4. L. M. Lansky, "Changing the Classroom: Some Psychological Assump-

tions," in *The Changing College Classroom,* ed. P. Runkel et al. (San Francisco: Jossey-Bass, 1969), pp. 293–301.

5. R. P. Wolff, "The Ideal of the University," *Change I* (September-October 1969): 48.

6. G. Trzebiatowski, "Educational Technology and the Elementary Teacher," in *Educational Comment 1969: Teacher Education in Context* (Toledo, Ohio: University of Toledo, 1969), pp. 64–86.

Competency Based

Teacher Education: 2

A Systems Approach
to Program Design

James M. Cooper
Wilford A. Weber
Charles E. Johnson

McCutchan Publishing Corporation
2526 Grove Street
Berkeley, California 94704

Contents

Contributors

Richard T. Coffing, Lecturer, School of Education, University of Massachusetts, Amherst, Massachusetts.

James M. Cooper, Associate Dean, College of Education, University of Houston, Houston, Texas.

M. Vere DeVault, Professor, Department of Curriculum and Instruction, University of Wisconsin, Madison, Wisconsin.

Norman R. Dodl, Associate Professor, Department of Elementary Education, Florida State University, Tallahassee, Florida.

Dale G. Hamreus, Research Professor, United States International University, San Diego, California.

Charles E. Johnson, Professor, College of Education, University of Georgia, Athens, Georgia.

John M. Kean, Associate Professor, Department of Curriculum and Instruction, University of Wisconsin, Madison, Wisconsin.

Charles Rathbone, Assistant Professor, Department of Education, University of Vermont, Burlington, Vermont.

H. Del Schalock, Research Professor, Oregon College of Education, Monmouth, Oregon.

Gilbert Shearron, Chairman, Elementary Education, College of Education, University of Georgia, Athens, Georgia.

Wilford A. Weber, Associate Professor, College of Education, University of Houston, Houston, Texas.

Introduction

A story is sometimes told about a mountain climber who was attempting to climb a previously unscaled mountain. After many days of superhuman effort, he arrived at the top of the mountain, scarred and bloody, but undaunted. Much to his dismay, he discovered that on the other side of the mountain a beautiful golden road led from the valley to the mountain's peak. The mountain climber returned to the valley via the road and proceeded to describe to the people of the valley the advantages of travelling the golden road.

In many respects this book represents the golden road. Many of the processes and procedures advocated for developing a competency based teacher education program are not those used by the authors as they developed their own model programs. The processes and procedures described represent those that the authors now advocate, rather than those initially used to scale the mountain. By describing the golden road approach we hope to spare our readers some of the scars and frustrations we encountered initially.

The purpose of this book is to help the reader design a competency based teacher education program using a systems approach. A competency based program is criteria referenced. By this we mean that the competencies to be demonstrated by the student and the criteria to be applied in assessing those competencies are made explicit, and students are held accountable for

1

demonstrating those competencies. Traditional teacher education programs are criteria based to the extent that prospective teachers are held accountable for the accumulation of credits taken in specific courses. The type of program around which this book is developed differs from traditional teacher education programs in its emphasis on demonstrated teacher competencies rather than successful completion of a series of courses.

As viewed in the present volume, teacher competencies may be assessed by using three types of criteria:

1. Teacher knowledge: facts, principles, generalizations, awareness, and sensitivities that the teacher is expected to acquire

2. Teacher performance: behaviors that the teacher is expected to demonstrate

3. Teacher consequences: outcomes that the teacher is expected to bring about in the emotional and intellectual growth of his pupils

These various kinds of teacher competencies are illustrated in the following diagram developed by H. Del Schalock.

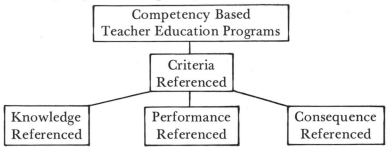

Thus, in a criteria referenced teacher education program the trainee is expected to demonstrate the possession of specific knowledge, which is the emphasis of most traditional programs; the ability to perform specific behavioral acts, which may be taken as evidence that certain skills or attitudes have been acquired; the ability to bring about the emotional or intellectual growth of pupils; or some combination of the three. In most criteria referenced programs trainees are asked to meet all three types of criteria, but most of these programs place the greatest emphasis on performance and consequence competencies.

The major point of emphasis is that in a competency based teacher education program certain objectives and criteria are unambiguously specified, and it is these criteria against which a teacher's competency can be measured. Rather than leaving the objectives and criteria vague, they are made as explicit as possible. Thus, the important consideration becomes whether the trainee demonstrates competency on specific criteria rather than whether he has taken a particular course.

The second major thrust of this book is the use of a systems approach to design and operate a competency based teacher education program. The systems approach is a composite of a number of planning, procedural, and allocative strategies that can be applied to designing an open, innovative, and person oriented teacher education program. A teacher education program can be viewed as a system of interrelated and interacting components that work in an integrated fashion to attain predetermined purposes.

This book is designed for current and prospective teacher educators, but it will not tell you what should be in the curriculum of a teacher education program or what instructional alternatives should be offered; its emphasis is on process. It is a "how-to-do-it" book, but it includes rationales for the procedures it advocates. The authors make two major assumptions: (1) that the program should be competency based; and (2) that a systematic approach should be used in planning, designing, and implementing the program. If you accept these assumptions, or are at least interested in their possibilities, this book should be helpful.

The genesis of this book can be traced to a project funded by the United States Office of Education: the Elementary Teacher Education Models Program. The project's task was to reconceptualize both preservice and inservice elementary teacher education. The nine institutions funded (a tenth—the University of Wisconsin—was added during the second phase of the project) developed the basic specifications for their models from 1 March 1968 to 31 October 1968. These institutions were: Teacher's College, Columbia University; Florida State University; University of Georgia; University of Massachusetts; Michigan State University; Northwest Regional Laboratory; Consortium of the State Universities of Ohio (The University of Toledo); University of Pittsburgh; Syracuse University; and the University of Wisconsin.

Two characteristics common to all the models were the systems approach used to design and operate the programs, and their competency based nature. Therefore, this book is based on the experiences of these ten institutions in designing their own elementary teacher education programs. It does not represent a composite of these programs; instead it outlines the process of using a systems approach to design and operate a competency based teacher education program. Since the audience for this book will include teacher educators representative of institutions of varying sizes, the authors have tried to provide representative examples of small and large teacher education programs.

Although aspects of a program can be transported, each institution must go through the process of designing its own program in its own environment if the program is to be accepted by the interested parties. The authors strongly believe that no teacher education model developed for one institution can be exported to another in its entirety. Therefore, this book emphasizes the process of design rather than the characteristics of a specific program. While no one model is generalizable in its entirety to other institutions, the design process is. If the reader wishes to focus on the content as well as the process, he is referred to the ten model elementary programs available from ERIC Clearinghouse on Teacher Education.

Chapter 1 examines some of the weaknesses of current teacher education programs and argues that many of these weaknesses can be overcome through the implementation of a systems designed, competency based teacher education program. Chapter 2 defines the systems approach, describes the decision-making process inherent in the systems approach, and indicates how both are used in designing a teacher education program.

Chapter 3 provides an overview of the curriculum-instruction design processes in a competency based teacher education program. Because curriculum-instruction is the heart of a teacher education program, a major portion of the book is devoted to these design processes. The first of these processes—the specification of program assumptions, goals, and objectives—is the focus of chapter 4. Chapter 5 emphasizes the necessity of maintaining congruence among program assumptions, goals, and objectives when designing competency based instructional processes.

Because the operation of a competency based teacher education program is a complex process, the need to manage the program effectively is great. Chapter 6 identifies the functions and activities associated with program management.

In addition to the curriculum-instruction aspects of a program, there are a number of support functions that must be performed if the program is to achieve its objectives. A description of several support functions is the focus of chapter 7.

A chief characteristic of a systems managed program is that its decisions are data based. Consequently, chapter 8 examines the processes related to assessing student progress and evaluating program effectiveness.

1

A Competency Based Systems Approach
to Teacher Education

James M. Cooper
Wilford A. Weber

Chapter Objectives

The reader will be able to (1) describe weaknesses of current teacher education programs, (2) describe how systems approaches can help correct these program weaknesses, (3) define the essential elements of a competency based teacher education program, and (4) define the essential elements of instructional modules.

Weaknesses of Current Teacher Education Programs

The critics of teacher education are many; they include public school personnel, prospective teachers enrolled in the programs, parents of children in schools, university professors, and social commentators. Many of the criticisms directed at teacher education programs are legitimate. It is always easier, of course, to criticize from a distance than it is from close up. Fault finding, however legitimate, by people who are not engaged in teacher education is often greeted by teacher educators with defensive and emotional reactions. It is not our purpose to either condemn or absolve teacher education; we are attempting to analyze some of its weaknesses and to propose certain solutions. We are directly involved in teacher education and have struggled continuously with the problems described. Our comments are meant to be constructive rather than accusatory.

Limited Conceptualization of the Total Program

Many teacher education programs are currently operated without comprehensive conceptualization. The faculties simply assume these programs will include a course in educational psychology, one in the philosophy or foundations of education, methods courses in particular curriculum areas, and a six-to-fifteen-week student-teaching experience. Very few programs are built on assumptions about the teacher's role within the school and the changing society or the kinds of skills and attitudes a teacher needs to grow continually as a person and teacher of children.

Should the teacher's primary role be to individualize instruction? Should the teacher be an innovator? Should success be measured by ability to bring about certain kinds of pupil outcomes? These questions are seldom asked. The concept of the teacher's role should suggest the structure and components of a program. The problem is that programs are too often constructed only in terms of courses that meet state certification requirements.

Lack of Research Base

Even if a program has been conceptualized in detail, it may not be based on a theoretical or research foundation. As research is conducted on teacher effectiveness, we are collecting more information about what an "effective" teacher is and does. As this information is generated, the findings should be used to improve program assumptions, goals, and instructional components. Until recently, research conclusions about teacher effectiveness were so skimpy that educators may have been somewhat justified in basing their programs on tradition and speculation. But this is no longer the case. Information on student teachers' needs can guide us in establishing priorities and sequencing their experiences, just as research on teacher directness and indirectness and the effects of their efforts on student attitudes and achievement suggests a model for teacher behavior in the classroom. Thus, a total teacher education program design must take into account this growing body of empirical knowledge.

Vaguely Defined Goals

Many teacher education programs operate year after year without specific goals or objectives. Even if a program has specifically stated goals, they are frequently so vague and general that, although they are easily accepted, they provide little direction for designing program components. General goals are necessary as broad guidelines for a program, but program planners need comprehensive, specifically stated outcomes that they wish to achieve. The planners can design a program that achieves its broad goals only by defining and designing program components to achieve them.

Piecemeal Changes and Innovations

In recent years a number of innovations, such as microteaching, interaction analysis, and simulation, have been introduced in teacher preparation programs. These innovations have great potential value, but too often they have simply been tacked onto an existing program with little or no adjustment in the rest of the program. The problem is that teacher educators do not view the teacher education program and its goals as an integrated system. Thus, they fail to consider (1) whether and how the innovation in question will help to achieve the program's goals, and (2) what effect the innovation will have on the other components of the system. This analytical failure sometimes results in wasteful overlap and disharmony among supposedly complementary components. At best the net result is that the addition of innovative practices does not significantly change the total program in the desired direction.

Program Components Determined by Tradition Rather than Function

In most schools of education the teacher education program is organized and administered by an elementary or secondary education department or a department of curriculum and instruction. As a new program is designed and developed, in all likelihood it will also be in one of these departments regardless of its nature or components. In effect, the departmental organization serves as a constraint on new functions if there are no qualified personnel to fulfill those functions within the department.

As new teacher education programs are designed, new functions will be called for and new roles will be developed. Not all of these roles will fit within the traditional teacher education departments. Some new roles will require such skills as evaluation, counseling, computer and media technology, and client analysis. In other words, the programs will require the performance of several interrelated tasks for which traditional curriculum and instruction departments are inadequately prepared.

Lack of Program Evaluation

The lack of specific objectives in most education programs contributes to yet another problem: the lack of programmatic evaluation processes for determining the degree to which program objectives are being met. If program objectives are not specified, it is clearly impossible to determine whether they are being achieved, because the degree to which objectives are made explicit determines the level of evaluation possible. Even when program objectives have been clearly specified, there has been a tendency to shy away from program evaluation, and when evaluation procedures have been employed, they have been focused on student progress rather than program effectiveness. It seems reasonable to suggest that this is a weakness that must be remedied.

Inadequate Data Base for Program Decisions

Just as the lack of specific objectives precludes effective program evaluation, poor program evaluation makes data based, programmatic decision making most difficult. A strong case can be made for the position that if a teacher education program is to be most effective in achieving its objectives, it must be continuously revised on the basis of constructive data supplied by sound evaluation procedures. Those responsible for making decisions must have access to data that permit them to determine which elements of the program warrant maintenance and which warrant change. Without such information, the program cannot improve and, in fact, deteriorates.

Unresponsiveness to Environmental Change

At least two factors contribute to this problem: (1) as suggested previously, program planners have rarely applied procedures for evaluating and using information regarding program effectiveness, and (2) teacher education institutions have tended to be closed systems assuming sole responsibility for the education of teachers. The solutions to the problem are implicit in these statements: (1) program planners must collect and use constructive data in program decision making, and (2) teacher education institutions must become equal partners with a wide range of organizations directly and indirectly concerned with teacher education, including the schools, the community, government educational agencies, professional organizations, education industries, and students. Only by sharing ideas with one another can we provide a climate in which responsiveness to social change is possible. Traditionally, teacher education programs have not needed to change rapidly, because society and its values have been fairly stable. The rapid social changes we are now experiencing require teacher education institutions to be far more responsive than ever before. Indeed, their ability to respond productively may be a crucial determinant of their future.

Lack of Client Orientation

Closely related to the notion that teacher education must take place in an open system is the notion that teacher education must become much more client oriented. Recent campus unrest makes this point all too clearly. It seems clear that student indictments of college programs as irrelevant are largely warranted. Future teacher education programs will surely be judged at least partially by their responsiveness to student demands for a voice in determining program content and process.

The teacher education student, however, is not the only client to which programs must be responsive. Pupils and the community at large must also be considered, since they are influenced by the behaviors of program graduates. Their direct involvement in program decision-making processes seems imperative.

Poor Models of Instruction

If "teach as they are taught" is a valid concept, and it seems reasonable to suggest that it is, teacher education programs have been guilty of passing on a "talk at 'em and give 'em the facts" approach to teachers. To find examples of this, we need only think of the college professor who lectures to two hundred students on "individualizing instruction" or uses a nonmedia presentation of "the appropriate uses of instructional media." It is a strong term, but *hypocrisy* is almost unavoidable in describing the present state of affairs. Clearly we need teacher education programs that reflect the instructional processes we would have teachers use in interaction with

children. Trite and obvious as it sounds, we must begin to practice
what we preach.

Use of Systems Approach to Help Correct Weaknesses

If the reader accepts the validity of the weaknesses mentioned
above, the question then becomes, How can these weaknesses be
overcome? The authors contend that most of these weaknesses can
be either solved or alleviated by applying new approaches to the
design of teacher education programs. Specifically, we believe that
the application of a systems approach to the design of criteria referenced, competency based teacher education programs would take
us a long way toward overcoming the problems cited above.

Definition of *System* and *Systems Approach*

Bela Banathy defines a *system* as a collection of interrelated and
interacting components that work in an integrated fashion to attain
predetermined purposes.[1] The human body, for example, is a physio-
logical system, the automobile a mechanical system, and the school a
social system.

The purpose of the system is realized through processes in which interacting
components of the system engage in order to produce a predetermined output.
Purpose determines the process required, and the process will imply the kinds of
components that will make up the system.[2]

The three features of purpose, processes, and components comprise a
way of analyzing, describing, and/or designing a teacher education
program. The application of such a systematic strategy to any human
process is called a *systems approach*. Most systems are product
oriented, that is, they operate in order to produce or accomplish
something. How accurately those products reflect the system's
purposes is the critical measure of the system's effectiveness.

The Systems Approach to Teacher Education Weaknesses

One can, and perhaps should, think of a teacher education program as a system. Its purpose is to develop teachers who possess
certain knowledge, behaviors, and attitudes that facilitate learning in
children. Its processes are the instructional experience a teacher
undergoes as he attempts to achieve identified knowledge, behaviors,

and attitudes that enable him to be an effective teacher of children. Its components are the managerial and instructional units (courses, learning modules, scheduling unit) necessary to organize and monitor the processes designed to achieve the program's purpose.

The products of the system are the teachers who graduate from the program. The primary measure of the program's success is whether these teachers have acquired the knowledge, behaviors, and attitudes the program has as its goals and whether they can bring about desired outcomes in their pupils. This implies that some sort of evaluation is necessary to ascertain the degree to which the teachers possess these competencies. The information derived from this evaluation is then fed back (hence, the term *feedback*) into the system in order to make any necessary alterations to the purposes, processes, or components of the program. When these corrections are made, the whole cycle is repeated again, becoming an ongoing regenerative process.

It is obvious that the program and its goals must be conceptualized in totality in order to determine the purposes, processes, and components. Thus, the systems approach forces a total look at the program's objectives, means, and subsystems and their relationships to one another.

The analytical process of the systems approach also encourages a theoretical and research base, because it forces the program to approach the education of teachers from a product oriented perspective. This calls for an evaluation of the available knowledge about teacher effectiveness and the learning process, how this knowledge can be used in designing the program, and what new knowledge is needed to produce the types of teachers desired. It is virtually impossible to design a program using a systems approach without reference to educational research and theory.

Goals and objectives are strongly affected by the systems approach. Objectives must be stated precisely, because the design of the processes and components depends on the objectives of the program. Program objectives are the criteria by which the system's effectiveness is judged. If the criteria are too vague, it is impossible objectively to evaluate the program's processes and components. Stated simply, if you don't know what you are trying to do, there is no way of finding out if you've done it.

In the past, teacher educators adopted a piecemeal approach to innovations in their programs; the systems approach forces planners to establish how these new practices relate to the goals and objectives of a program. The fact that something is new and others are trying it is no longer justification for its adoption. It must be considered in relation to the program's purposes, processes, and components, because all the elements of the program are interrelated and affect one another. Changing one element of the program will have some effect on the other elements, and this fact must be recognized.

In teacher education, program components have traditionally been established as departmental structures, which generally lack flexibility and adaptability. When a new program is instituted the departmental structure rarely changes significantly. Thus, the components cannot be designed specifically to facilitate the achievement of the program's objectives. If teacher educators use a systems approach to design the program, this discrepancy becomes obvious and the components can be reorganized.

The basic concepts of a systems approach are not new. The ideas have been around and applied for a long time, although the current terminology is relatively new. The ideas and processes have even been applied in education, but until recently they have not found their way into teacher education. There is nothing mystical about the systems approach; it is a logical and analytical process. However, it will require teacher educators to acquire a new vocabulary and accept a new approach to the design of a program. The new language and the complex processes will discourage some from adopting this approach to teacher education. But unless we can understand a system, including teacher education and its relation to the whole of education, we can neither justify our current practices nor recommend changes.

The Competency Based Teacher Education Program

Definition

A competency based teacher education program specifies the competencies to be demonstrated by the student, makes explicit the criteria to be applied in assessing the student's competencies, and holds the student accountable for meeting those criteria. While at first glance this definition appears to depict a rather harsh, almost mechanistic process, nothing could be further from the truth. The competencies referred to are attitudes, understandings, skills, and behaviors that facilitate intellectual, social, emotional, and physical growth in children. The student is held responsible for demonstrating these competencies, because they are necessary to teaching effectiveness. He may, however, help to determine either the competencies to be acquired, or the setting in which the competencies are to be demonstrated, or both. Three types of criteria are used to determine the student's level of achievement in these competencies: (1) knowledge criteria, which are used to assess the cognitive understandings of the student; (2) performance criteria, which are used to assess the teaching behaviors of the student; and (3) consequence criteria, which are used to assess the student's teaching effectiveness by examining the emotional and intellectual growth of his pupils.

Teacher Effectiveness Research

Competency based teacher education programs provide excellent opportunities for identifying appropriate teacher competencies through process-product research, that is, research that attempts to relate observed teacher behaviors to student outcome measures. While several competency based teacher education programs have been developed, the relationship between the specified competencies that the teachers are to demonstrate and the desired changes in their students' behaviors has yet to be established. In general, these competencies represent experienced teacher educators' opinions regarding the knowledge and skills a prospective teacher should possess, but these educators would be hard-pressed to defend their criteria from a research base.

While applauding the U.S. Office of Education's development of the Elementary Teacher Education Models Program and their emphasis on performance criteria or competencies, certain educational researchers note the absence of research data to guide teacher educators in designing their programs. At the same time, these researchers argue that performance or competency based programs offer ". . . ways to increase our knowledge of the relationship between these specific teacher behaviors and measures of pupil achievement."[3] The validity of performance criteria or competencies can be ascertained by conducting experiments to determine whether teachers trained in specific competencies behave differently in their classrooms from similar teachers who did not receive such training. When we have also identified teaching behaviors that relate strongly to pupil outcomes, teacher education will have a research base that can lead to improved training programs.

Desirable Characteristics of Competency Based Programs

There are several essential characteristics of a teacher education program that the authors advocate. One of these is personalized instruction. By this we mean active involvement of the prospective teacher in making choices based on consideration of the personal relevance of what is to be learned. The flexibility of the competency based program should allow students a choice of goals and objectives, thus increasing their chances of becoming independent, self-directed, and continuing learners and providing models that enable them to translate the principles and processes of personalized instruction to the education of their pupils.

Another desirable characteristic of a teacher education program is emphasis on fieldwork. The trend in teacher education is to place increasing emphasis on the use of performance and product criteria and less reliance on the traditional knowledge, or course completion, criterion. There seems to be increasing acceptance of the notion that what teachers know about teaching in no way assures their ability to teach or foster growth in children. Competency based programs tend to be reality oriented; the students spend a great deal of time in the schools interacting with children, and many of their competencies are evaluated in that setting.

In a traditional program time is held constant, and achievement varies. That is, the program is set within a certain time limit—usually four years—and students go through an established number of courses and are required to obtain a particular number of credits and a minimum grade point average. The emphasis is on the completion of the courses regardless of whether the student has acquired mastery in all areas of study. On the other hand, in a competency based program achievement is held constant in a sense, and time varies. The program specifies the criteria levels at which competencies are achieved, and the student moves through the program at his own rate; he moves as quickly as he wishes and is able.

Traditional programs heavily emphasize program entrance re-

quirements, while competency based programs emphasize exit requirements. A competency based approach seems to be particularly
advantageous to those who have been denied equal educational
opportunity and, because of the usual entrance requirements, might
not otherwise be given a chance. It seems more logical to look at an
individual's abilities after he has completed a program than before he
has entered it. Another obvious advantage is the assurance such an
approach gives regarding the achievement of mastery in all specified
areas by all graduates.

At the very heart of the competency based teacher education
program is the instructional module. An instructional module can be
defined as a set of learning activities intended to facilitate the
learner's acquisition and demonstration of a particular competency
or particular competencies.

In simple terms, an instructional module may be thought of as
comprising:

1. A rationale that (a) describes the purpose and importance of
the objectives of the module in empirical, theoretical, and/or practical terms; and (b) places the module and the objectives of the
module within the context of the total program

2. Objectives that specify the competency or competencies the
student is expected to demonstrate

3. Prerequisites, i.e., any competencies the student should have
prior to entering the module

4. Preassessment procedures—usually diagnostic in nature—that
provide the student with an opportunity to demonstrate mastery of
the objectives or relevant to the objectives

5. Learning alternatives, which are the various instructional
options available to the student and each of which is designed to
contribute to his acquisition of the objectives

6. Postassessment procedures that permit the student to demonstrate achievement of the objectives

7. Remedial procedures to be undertaken with students who are
unable to demonstrate achievement of the objectives on the postassessment.

A number of things about the various elements of the module
are worthy of emphasis.

1. The objective or objectives are made public.

2. The preassessment provides the student with an opportunity

to demonstrate competencies he already possesses and the option to bypass the instructional activities relevant to those competencies he has demonstrated.

3. Both the preassessment and postassessment should be reality oriented, that is, the testing situation should be as close to the "real thing" as is possible. Therefore, performance and product criteria are frequently used to assess student progress.

4. Most important, a modular approach increases possibilities for self-pacing, individualization, personalization, independent study, and alternative means of instruction: an obvious advantage.

In summary, we are convinced that the most attractive response to the program weaknesses cited earlier is a competency based teacher education program incorporating aspects of the other new trends in teacher education, such as a systems approach, personalized instruction, interdisciplinary curricula, multi-institutional patterns of organization, differentiated staffing patterns, and new technology. We believe that competency based teacher education holds great promise and deserves adequate testing.

Footnotes

1. Bela Banathy, *Instructional Systems* (Palo Alto: Fearon Publishers, 1968), p. 4.
2. Banathy, *Instructional Systems*, p. 12.
3. Barak Rosenshine & Norma Furst, "Research on Teacher Performance Criteria," in *Research in Teacher Education*, B. Othanel Smith, ed. (Englewood Cliffs, N.J.: Prentice-Hall, 1971), p. 65.

2

Systems Approach Applications in Designing Teacher Education Programs

M. Vere DeVault

Chapter Objectives

The reader will be able to (1) clarify the nature of systems approaches as they relate to teacher education programs, and (2) identify systems procedures for managing the design process of teacher education programs.

The Systems Approach and Teacher Education

Major changes have been made in teacher education in the past two decades. Improved certification procedures, increased concern and emphasis on the interdisciplinary nature of and responsibility for teacher education, more realistic approaches to the clinical experience, and improved use of media and technology are all trademarks of evolving teacher education programs through the fifties and sixties.

Notwithstanding these improvements, the gap between what teacher education is and what it must be is greater than ever before. John W. Gardner has said, "The pieces of the educational revolution are lying around unassembled." A major task confronting teacher education, then, is one of putting those pieces together both to ensure that each contributes to overall objectives in a systematic way and to determine the extent to which those pieces are, indeed, necessary for effective teacher education. To achieve this purpose of systematically relating a wide variety of bits and pieces into a smoothly functioning whole, education is turning to systems approaches.

Defining the Systems Approach

Banathy provides a series of statements that are useful in conceptualizing the meaning of the systems approach.

> The roots of the systems approach are set in the scientific method and it has emerged from an eclectic use of principles from such diverse fields as logic, philosophy, psychology, cybernetics, and other disciplines. Its orderly design of procedures and strategies, its approach to the selection and integration of resources, its insistence upon optimization of functions and components appear to be characterized by common sense. In fact, the shortest definition which can be suggested for the systems approach is that it is common sense by design.[1]

Someplace between Banathy's concept of systems approach as "an eclectic use of principles from such diverse fields as logic, philosophy, psychology, cybernetics, and other disciplines," and his "common sense" idea is his statement, mentioned in chapter 1, about the purpose of systems. This statement will serve as our working definition of the systems approach:

> The purpose of the system is realized through processes in which interacting components of the system engage in order to produce a predetermined output. Purpose determines the process required, and the process will imply the kinds of components that will make up the system.

Purposes

Purpose is simply that which a system intends to accomplish. In a teacher education program, therefore, the purpose is to graduate a teacher who is capable of teaching children effectively.

If the purposes of a teacher education program are to be realized through processes interacting with components, these purposes, processes, and components must be carefully determined. Purposes in teacher education programs are expressed in statements of goals and objectives at several levels of specificity. Chapter 4 discusses in detail the processes for determining assumptions, goals, and objectives for teacher education programs.

Processes

Processes are operations that are intended to achieve the purposes of a system. In a teacher education program the processes include the instructional activities the student experiences with the expectation that these contribute to his becoming an effective teacher.

In decades past, the processes involved to achieve the purposes of teacher education programs were few in number and relatively similar from one program to another. Universally accepted were classroom lecturing, reading and writing assignments, examinations, and observing and brief periods of student teaching in real classrooms. More recently, teacher education programs may be characterized as having a greater variety of processes, including individualizing instruction, microteaching, human relations training, role playing, cooperating with community agencies, simulating, continuous in-school experience, managing, monitoring student progress, allocating resources, and budgeting funds for development activities. Naturally, not all of these processes are used by each subsystem, since the purposes of each subsystem are different.

Components

Components are the working parts of a system and are dictated by the processes required in order to achieve the purposes of a system. That is, they are the resources that interact to create processes designed to achieve the system purpose. In a teacher education program, components include instructors, instructional hardware and software, and educational facilities.

Process to a large extent implies the nature of the components to be included in the teacher education program. If individualizing instruction is an important process, for example, management components will be needed to provide for continuous monitoring of student progress; if teaching in seminars and large-group instruction is a desired process, adequate physical facilities comprise necessary components; if microteaching processes are to be used, learning modules must be designed that effectively incorporate that process.

Evaluation; Feedback

The purpose of a system is measured in terms of its product, usually called its output. In a teacher education program the major output is a teacher who it is hoped has achieved the knowledge, attitudes, and skills that the program aimed to develop. The major input of a teacher education program is the student entering the program, along with the resources available for training. Instructional processes must be developed to help him achieve the competencies he lacks. These instructional processes, as well as all the support and management functions necessary to achieve the purposes of the system, are the processes or operations of the system.

If a system is to maintain itself, it must ensure the adequacy of its output. This means the teacher education program must continually assess the degree to which its graduates possess the desired competencies and adjust the system accordingly. The program must also treat the desired competencies as assumptions whose relationships to pupil outcomes must be validated. The assessment is fed back into the system, hence the term *feedback*. The relationship between input operations or processes, output, and feedback is illustrated in figure 1.

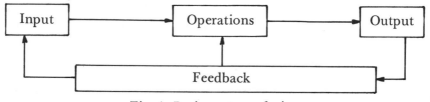

Fig. 1. Basic systems design

Subsystems

Once the goals and objectives of the main system have been specified, it is necessary to describe the major subsystems. A subsystem is an operational entity within a system, capable of functioning independently or of permitting independent design and analysis. Subsystems are so defined as to represent the major processes or operations within the system. Each subsystem description contains information on the resources required for its operation. Most significantly, like the main system, each subsystem is described in terms of its purposes, processes, components.

The selection of subsystems depends on the type of program being designed. Possible subsystems within a teacher education program might include:

1. A curriculum-instructional subsystem organized on the basis of specific instructional objectives, instructional processes, and personnel. Although each instructional module in the subsystem could be designed independently, each must be compatible with the others

and with the overall purposes of the total teacher education program system.

2. A management subsystem whose functions might include solving organizational problems; allocating the funds for the program; supplying the instructional subsystems with the necessary materials, staff, and paraprofessionals necessary to operate the program; and coordinating the program with the rest of the university and with other agencies involved.

3. An information subsystem whose function might be to maintain files indicating the current status of all resources, including staff, facilities, and equipment. The data contained in this subsystem could include (a) the cost in terms of resources, the student and faculty time required to help each student meet each competency, and the instructional route chosen; and (b) the system status of each trainee, i.e., what competencies he has met.

4. An evaluation subsystem whose function would be to monitor program effectiveness and to assess student performance by gathering feedback regarding the quality, success, competency, acceptability, and competitiveness of the program's graduates. This feedback could be used to add, delete, and modify instructional modules, thus assuring that the program monitors its success in achieving its goals.

Management Processes for Designing Competency Based Teacher Education Programs

Commitment to a competency based systems approach to the teacher education program implies a parallel commitment to the use of a systems approach in designing the program. Likewise, at all levels—from deans, superintendents, and administration-faculty-student committees concerned with institutional policy decisions, to the individual faculty member responsible for decisions about instructional alternatives—a clear commitment to a decision-making strategy is essential to the effective functioning of a systems approach. Management by a systems approach assumes a continuing flow of pertinent data and the identification of specific points at which designated individuals or groups of persons make decisions. A useful way of perceiving the relationship between data processing and decision making is represented in figure 2.

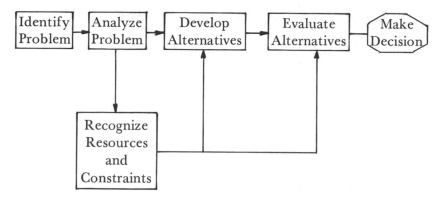

Fig. 2. Decision-making procedure within a systems approach

Let us consider briefly an illustrative problem using the decision-making chart shown in figure 2. Assume that we have identified our problem as that of deciding who should determine the teaching competencies expected of program graduates. The first task is to analyze the process for which we are creating a design.

Questions to be examined include: Who is now involved in this process? What persons now omitted from the process should be involved? What advantages and disadvantages accrue from their involvement? What are the consequences if they are not involved?

The next task is to identify alternative solutions to the given problem. A key to the effectiveness of systems management is the quality of the alternatives provided the decision maker. Major creative efforts are required in developing these alternatives. The present example implies a great many possible alternatives, including situations in which teacher educators (1) are solely responsible for the specification of competencies; (2) are responsible for the specification of competencies while accepting inputs from a wide range of advisory groups; or (3) share the responsibility with representatives from a wide range of groups. Of course, many additional alternatives may be considered at this point. However, each of them must be carefully considered, keeping the existing resources and constraints well in mind.

The development of alternatives, then, requires not only creative effort and a clear notion of purpose but also a realistic recognition of resources and constraints. One such resource/constraint factor is the competence of the present or available staff. If the staff is not presently competent to make a needed contribution, can it attain this competence? Does the staff have the will to attain competence, and are there any rewards for its attainment that are likely to encourage the staff in this direction? Alternatives must also be realistic in terms of existing or available facilities and finances. If computers may help but are not generally available, are there alternatives that do not require computers? Are the necessary commitments from various partners substantial enough to support long-range planning? If not, in what ways can the alternative be adapted to the range of commitments on which one can depend?

Every resource is finite and thus implies a constraint. As these resource/constraint characteristics are identified, they are used to sort through the several desirable alternatives and select the few that may be supported for long-term program development. Each of these should be carefully described and supported with a set of statements indicating its particular advantages and disadvantages. When the alternatives have been developed with the resources and constraints in mind, the decision maker can evaluate the alternatives and select the one that is thought will be the most effective and efficient in solving the problem.

Given the decision-making procedure illustrated in figure 2, the next essential step is to make certain that the decision maker has been clearly identified. To whom will the alternatives be presented? When the responsible individual or group has been identified, it must be delegated and, if necessary, trained to assume that responsibility. Because decision making goes on at a number of levels—policy, management, or instruction—the decision-making procedure discussed in the paragraphs above can be applied at each of these levels, and at each level both the purpose and the decision maker must be clearly identified.

Essential Steps in the Design Process

For the purpose of this description, it is assumed that the initial decision makers have been identified and that they have decided to adopt a systems approach to management. Let us now consider a series of steps through which teacher educators may wish to proceed in the development of a model design for a teacher education program.

Determining Purposes

Decisions must be made concerning the purpose of the teacher education program. Although this seems at first to be somewhat obvious—a kind of routine busywork—such is not the case. Is the program to be designed for the purpose of preparing a specific number of teachers, or is it to be flexible enough to accommodate as many candidates as seek admission and meet requirements? Is the program to be designed for the purpose of preparing a single kind of teacher, for instance, at the elementary school level, or is it to serve the preparation needs of specialists as well? Is the program to be continuous from admission to retirement, or is it to be a preservice preparation program? These and similar questions must be answered as the purposes of the program are defined. There are five steps in the development of a set of purposes that are to give direction to the design of the teacher education program.

1. Identify the several institutions and individuals that should be involved in determining the purposes to be served by the teacher education program. The systems approach to the preparation of teachers implies that relationships are developed among all institutions having responsibilities for aspects of program development or operation. To assure commitment to program goals, these cooperating agencies or institutions must be identified early so that their representatives can be participants in the determination of purposes. In addition to the value of ideas from a variety of sources or points of view, early involvement results in a sense of cooperative and continuing participation in the program. Institutions that should be considered at this earliest date include the local schools in which students either serve as student teachers, interns, or beginning teachers; the several departments, divisions, or faculties on campus that have some responsibility for planning or instruction in the teacher education program; the state department of education; and professional education organizations and teachers' unions.

2. Determine data resources that are important to the delineation of the teacher education program purposes. Data about the nature of students presently entering or expected to enter the institution is of major importance to the work of the committee. Likewise, the committee needs data on the nature of school positions that

students are expected to assume after certification. The needs of the state or region must be carefully surveyed as part of the data available to this committee. It is unlikely that a college or university located far from a major urban setting will be an appropriate place to build a program focused primarily on the preparation of teachers for inner-city schools. On the other hand, it is frequently true that local schools with special student populations have been largely ignored by teacher preparation institutions in their locality. Each institution's resources, staff and facilities must be investigated to determine their impact on the ability of the institution to serve a given purpose.

3. Once the data are available, identify several alternative statements of purpose for the teacher education program. The group should explore a large number of potential alternatives. The greater the variety of alternatives that are explored, the more fruitful the final decision making is likely to be, even though it is probable that only two or three alternatives will ultimately be submitted to the major decision-making body. Initially, a great variety of alternatives should be suggested, listed, studied, analyzed, and then accepted or rejected.

4. Refine two or more alternative statements of purpose for presentation to the decision-making body. In the collection and discussion of numerous alternatives, two or three will usually stand out as the strongest of possibilities. Each of these should be prepared carefully in writing as a separate and complete document and should be accompanied by an objective assessment of its advantages and disadvantages. This assessment should consider resources and constraints and environmental criteria in association with the data collected in step 2.

5. Make a decision concerning the alternatives submitted. (This is done by the major decision-making body.) This decision may be to accept one of the alternatives presented by the committee, to bring together parts of two or more of the alternatives, or to return to the committee a request for additional clarification or new alternatives if those presented seem unacceptable.

Once a statement of purposes has been carefully designed and a decision has been made that these purposes clearly identify the direction to be undertaken by the developing teacher education program, it becomes necessary to conceptualize the subsystems needed to achieve the program's goals. The program designers follow the steps outlined above to establish a set of purposes, processes, and components for each subsystem.

Determining Processes

When each subsystem's objectives have been determined, the processes for achieving these purposes must be decided. Again, the five basic steps provide direction for systematic management.

1. Determine the individuals responsible for identifying processes to be employed in implementing the purposes selected. In many instances it will be appropriate for the same individuals who determined the subsystem's purposes to determine the processes and components to follow. Ideally, these individuals will be representatives of the groups that will be responsible for the development and operation of the processes of the subsystem.

2. Collect data—through a survey of literature, present practice, and projected future programs—to determine appropriate processes that are available or being planned throughout the education community.

3. Once the data described in step 2 are available, identify several alternative general ideas about process. Familiarity with processes being used and developed is essential at this point. A committee not completely familiar with these processes may provide alternatives that fail to serve purposes as well as possible. Lack of this essential data might also result in the selection of processes that have already proven less effective than others in meeting the purposes identified.

If the curriculum-instruction subsystem's major purpose is the preparation of teachers recruited from practicing paraprofessionals throughout a large state or region, for example, the processes employed may be quite unusual. To facilitate maximum study by working paraprofessionals, it may be necessary to initiate telelecturing from a campus to several locations throughout a state at the same time. A program designed simultaneously to serve the community and prepare participants for certification may require meeting in small groups or individual instruction in schools or community settings for much of the preparation program. On the other hand, a combination of individualized learning, class discussion, and traditional classroom teaching may serve the purposes of many programs.

Processes that include such activities as counseling, recruiting, instructing, microteaching, intern teaching, writing, and assessing may all be included in any given program. At this point the curriculum-instruction subsystem committee's task is not to select from among these, deleting some and accepting others, but to determine which processes are most appropriate to the program's purposes. Thus, any alternative proposal concerning the processes to be employed in a subsystem will include a number of suggestions, and a major task will be to identify clearly what relationship among these processes is likely to be needed to achieve the purposes of the subsystem.

4. Develop in detail two or more alternatives, including statements of their advantages and disadvantages, for presentation to the decision-making body. For each purpose, a set of alternative processes are to be identified, refined, and submitted to the appropriate decision-making body. Thus, the decision-making procedure is repeatedly implemented as processes (and components) are identified for each purpose within the system.

5. Decide which processes are to be used to implement the purposes both of the subsystem and of the program.

Determining Components

Having identified the processes by which purposes are to be achieved, the next task is to determine the components that will be required for each subsystem.

1. Determine the individuals responsible for identifying the manner in which the subsystem's components will be organized. Again, it may be expected that the individuals who were responsible for the identification of purposes and processes will also be responsible for the determination of components. This is not necessarily the case, however, and careful attention must be given to this decision. Information about alternative component designs may be supplied by different individuals from those concerned with purposes and processes, and the difference may dictate a different decision-making group.

2. Collect data concerning the components necessary to operate the processes that have already been determined.

3. If possible, identify several alternative components for each desired process.

4. Develop in detail two or more alternatives, with statements concerning their advantages and disadvantages (including cost and

availability), for presentation to the decision-making body.

5. Decide which components are most appropriate and feasible for each process required to achieve the purposes of the subsystem.

This cycle of five steps for each of the systems requirements—purposes, processes, and components—has focused on the higher levels of the system and subsystem design. It has been concerned with the processes of decision-making that typically reside with presidents, deans, superintendents, and faculty-teacher-student committees. Decisions at other levels will be made by other appropriate individuals or groups of individuals, as in departments or teams of instructional personnel. At the lowest level, someone will be responsible for making a decision about a single instructional activity: its purpose, the processes by which that purpose is to be achieved, and the components that are to be used in the achievement of that purpose. To achieve the purpose associated with a single activity may call for observation of some student activity, and the component identified for use in this observation may be a commercially available film. Whether the decision is made by a single faculty member or teacher or by a larger group will likely depend on the permanence with which that decision is expected to dictate the learning alternatives available to students. If that activity is part of a single course, a single professor may well make the decision; if it is part of a bank of instructional activities available to learners, a larger group is likely to be identified as the decision maker. Figure 3 graphically depicts the steps discussed above.

A warning is appropriate at this point. The systems approach is not a simple linear activity. Many processes and components interact, and feedback from any point can force reexamination of an earlier step before proceeding further. This process of reiteration is extremely important. Too frequently, concentration on the step-by-step nature of the systems approach prevents appreciation of the degree to which a later act can influence the rethinking of an earlier step. Information from operation is used to evaluate the adequacy of the system description. Communication between subsystems should serve as a basis for adjusting the operation of both. The effective implementation of systems procedures requires the development of feedback mechanisms to permit adjustments at all critical points of the system.

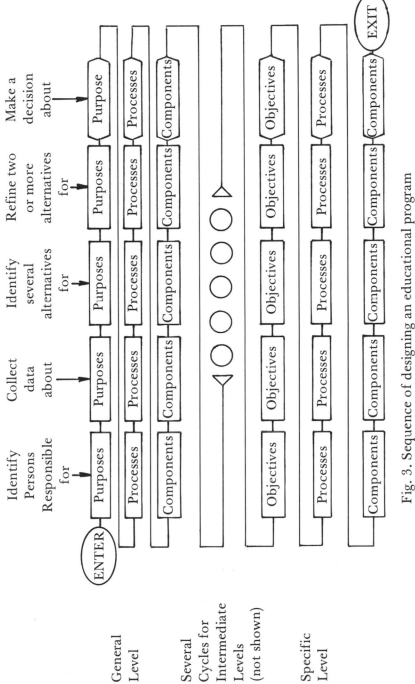

Fig. 3. Sequence of designing an educational program

Conclusion

The systems approach can be viewed as a philosophy of organization and management. There is ample evidence to indicate that systems designs can substantially benefit the management and organization of complex undertakings. Although much is still unknown about the benefits and problems associated with systems in education, the complexity of problems in educational innovation and change is being recognized now as it has never been recognized before. With this recognition has come an interest in the potential benefits of systems approaches to the solution of educational problems. The discussions and procedures recommended in this chapter are provided in the hope that readers will see ways in which these ideas may be adapted to the solution of management and organizational problems in their local educational settings. Obviously, the suggestions here are presented in simplistic terms. What is not so obvious is the manner in which these ideas can be adapted for implementation in the day-to-day solution of problems. Systems approaches to educational problems do not themselves provide solutions. It is expected, however, that the context of systems approaches will facilitate the solutions of educational problems. Implementation of the ideas expressed throughout this chapter will require the dedicated, intelligent, and creative leadership that has always been characteristic of those who successfully bring about changes in social institutions.

Footnotes

1. Bela H. Banathy, "The Design of Foreign Language Teacher Education," *The Modern Language Journal* 52, no. 8 (December 1968): 491.

3

A Systems Approach to Curriculum Development

John M. Kean

Norman R. Dodl

Chapter Objectives

The reader will be able to (1) describe a systems approach to curriculum-instruction development in a teacher education program, (2) identify the major functions of the curriculum-instruction design processes, and (3) identify the major decision points in the curriculum-instruction design process.

Introduction

This chapter describes a systems approach to curriculum-instruction development in a teacher education program. In most teacher education programs the curriculum-instruction aspect is generally considered to be the whole program. Although curriculum-instruction is the heart of the program, it is but one subsystem of the total program. The design of this curriculum-instruction subsystem is the focus of this and the next two chapters.

Curriculum has been defined in various ways, but the definition used here is: the sum of all the instructional objectives and concomitant learning experiences offered to the learner. In teacher education, the major goal is to produce teachers who possess the knowledge, attitudes, and skills that the program designers deem necessary to facilitate children's learning. The teacher education curriculum consists of objectives and learning experiences designed to help prospective teachers achieve the specified competencies. A systems approach facilitates more comprehensive curriculum planning, allows for better integration of components, and forces greater flexibility in selecting procedures for achieving program goals. Systematic planning allows us to reach for educational goals, apply our theories, validate our procedures, and exercise our professional judgments in ways that less systematic approaches seemingly do not allow.

When using a systems approach, we must still consider the traditional questions of curriculum design. We must deal with the needs of the individual, the nature and needs of society, a system of values, objectives, type and organization of content, scope, sequencing, methods, media, and evaluation.[1]

Curriculum-Instruction Design Processes

The systems oriented curriculum-instruction design process can be construed as a series of functions that must be performed to achieve the objectives of the subsystem. Each function includes identifiable processes and products. The functions of a curriculum-instruction subsystem are:

1. Specification of assumptions, goals, and objectives
2. Generation and selection of objective criteria
3. Identification and design of assessment strategies
4. Specification of instructional philosophy
5. Development of instructional strategies
6. Selection and/or development of instructional resources
7. Development of feedback mechanisms

Specification of Assumptions, Goals, and Objectives

The first task in the design process is to identify the assumptions, goals, and objectives of the curriculum-instruction subsystem. It is explicit in the systems approach that people of diverse vested interests, rhetorical and ideological concepts, and differentiated expertise must be involved in the development of the program if the objectives are to be reality based.[2] Thus, objectives should be defined by the cooperative endeavors of university faculty and representatives from other education institutions, such as public schools, community schools, free schools, and state departments of education; potential teachers; and the communities, children, and parents who are the "consumers" of the program product: the teacher.

Moreover, this identification of objectives is not based on knowledge or discipline orientations alone. The group defining the objectives must be guided by the best available knowledge about what makes an effective teacher, that is, one who functions in the life space of the community in which he teaches and helps both the community and its children create a better life. There is a wide variety of data sources, including published materials, identified problems, and common expectancies of client populations.

Most teacher education programs are organized into courses that are subject matter or discipline oriented, for example, educational psychology, social studies, and science. If the curriculum-instruction subsystem is initially organized according to these divisions, the objectives produced will reflect the subject matter orientations. In other words, the structure of the subject matter and the mind set of the individuals involved will *a priori* dictate the kinds of curriculum-instruction objectives produced. If, on the other hand, the group organized to identify objectives is interdisciplinary and includes prospective teachers, parents, public school personnel, and community representatives, the objectives identified will most likely be quite different. Who is involved and how they are initially organized to select the subsystem's objectives will determine the output of the subsystem, that is, what kinds of knowledge, attitudes, and skills the graduates of the program will possess.

The major task of determining the objectives of the curriculum-instruction subsystem, then, can be done in two different ways:

1. Determine *a priori* the subsystems and their general purpose, and organize separate task forces to select the objectives for each of the subsystems.

2. Organize task forces to select the objectives, and then organize the objectives into the curriculum on the basis of their similarities.

The advantage of the first approach is that major overlaps and gaps may be avoided by initially conceptualizing the major subsystems. The reader may discover that as a result of the specification of objectives process, it may become necessary to reconceptualize the subsystems. The advantage of the second approach is the greater likelihood that it will produce more creative approaches to curriculum organization. Whichever process is used, objectives are organized into subsystems based on similar purpose. Chapter 4 describes in more detail the process for identifying assumptions, goals, and objectives and their relationships to one another.

The way objectives are determined will influence the way these objectives are eventually organized into the curriculum. If subject matter specialists are organized to select objectives, it is very likely that the objectives they select will be grouped according to subject matter in the curriculum. If other approaches for organizing the curriculum are desired, different mixes of people must be delegated to select objectives.

Generation and Selection of Objective Criteria

In order to evaluate the student vis-à-vis the objectives that have been generated, it is necessary to specify what indicators will be accepted as evidence that the objectives have been achieved. In teacher education programs it is necessary to specify the knowledge, performance skills, and consequences of the prospective teacher's behavior that must be demonstrated as evidence that the objective has been achieved. In some instances, these criteria can be specified in advance by the same individuals who are involved in selecting the objectives. In other instances, the criteria may be individually negotiated with the students. In either case, the task is to make each objective operational.

A variety of information sources will be consulted in specifying outcome criteria. The group involved in this process will present a variety of outcome criteria to the decision makers, who can then make selections for use in the various parts of the teacher education program.

Identification and Design of Assessment Strategies

It may be best to have the assessment procedures set up by design teams including such people as measurement and evaluation specialists. The value of these procedures, however, rests on acceptance by all parties concerned. For this reason, students, community representatives, and professionals must share the responsibility of choosing acceptable assessment procedures from the data provided by the professional team.

The assessment strategies must be appropriate for the specific objective. If the objective requires that the student demonstrate the acquisition of knowledge, then written tests, interviews, and discussions are appropriate assessment procedures. If the objective requires that the student demonstrate a performance skill, appropriate assessment procedures might include microteaching, simulation exercises, and actual teaching. If the objective requires that the student demonstrate the ability to bring about specific changes in pupils, assessment would require actual teaching situations in which the desired pupil changes can be measured.

The program must develop the capacity to monitor student progress continuously in order to aid the student in modifying his own program structure and perhaps even his objectives. Such diagnosis requires information and evaluation subsystems allowing data storage and rapid retrieval of student profiles. Finally, because there is a need for program evaluation as well as student assessment, data must be gathered during all phases of the program and beyond in order to assess the effectiveness of graduates in the classroom and the program's effect on students. Both student and program evaluation are discussed in more detail in Chapter 8.

Specification of Instructional Philosophy

Marshall McLuhan's often-quoted phrase, "the medium is the message," should be a guiding principle for program designers. Many educators argue that the processes and structure of instruction impinge more directly and influentially on learners than the objectives themselves. The position taken here is that both the objectives selected and the instructional processes designed greatly influence the teacher's eventual performance. Consequently, the instructional processes used in educating the teacher should model the processes the program designers want him to use in his own teaching. For example, if the teacher is expected to individualize instruction for the pupils, the teacher education program must be individualized. In short, as program designers conceptualize the role of the teacher through the specification of program assumptions and goals, that conceptualization must be reflected in the program's instructional philosophy. That instructional philosophy dictates the instructional processes that are congruent with the program's assumptions about the teacher's role. The day of lecturing about discovery learning should be over.

Development of Instructional Strategies

Once the assessment contexts have been designed, a team should take over the responsibility of designing strategies to enable students to achieve each objective. Based on the earlier identification and selection of objectives, the task analysis consists of creating and assessing what actually must happen in order to accomplish the objectives already specified.

For example, if the objective requires the student to demonstrate the ability to ask probing questions, a task analysis would attempt to identify the knowledge and/or skills the student would have to possess in order to ask probing questions. Such a task analysis reveals, among other things, that the student would have to know what probing questions were, why they are useful, and when they should be used. If properly executed, a task analysis of each objective greatly aids the staff in preparing appropriate learning alternatives, thus increasing the chances that more students will eventually be able to demonstrate the competency. For complex competencies, the task analysis should identify a set of objectives and various appropriate learning alternatives. This process leads to an incremental approach to the achievement of the competencies specified. Chapter 5 presents a more detailed description of the processes of designing and selecting an instructional philosophy, instructional strategies, and instructional resources.

Selection and/or Development of Instructional Resources

Once the learning alternatives have been identified, the selection and/or development of appropriate instructional resources becomes important. This task is best accomplished by the same people who were involved in the specification of the instructional philosophy and strategies, because congruence among philosophy, strategies, and resources is crucial. It is presumed here that no team in a single program can create all of the instructional resources needed for the program; materials will be obtained from a variety of sources, such as the ERIC Clearinghouses, commercial producers, and other teacher education programs. It is important that these materials be judged and, when necessary, adapted to fit the needs and requirements of the particular objectives for which they have been selected. For example, a film designed to illustrate the concept of positive verbal reinforcement might also illustrate the concept of asking probing questions. Thus, the film might be used by program designers to illustrate the concept of asking probing questions rather than the concept for which it was initially designed. In all cases, instructional resources should be viewed as alternatives that are made available to help students achieve particular objectives. The construction and selection of instructional resources is dictated by the nature of the objectives; the availability of materials should not dictate the selection of program objectives.

Development of Feedback Mechanisms

A curriculum-instruction subsystem should be regenerative, that is, feedback mechanisms must be built into the subsystem to assess the adequacy of objectives, instructional strategies, and other operations of the subsystem so that necessary adjustments can be made. Because neither society nor client needs are static and unchanging, this type of feedback is imperative if the curriculum-instruction subsystem is to be dynamic and growing. Chapter 8 discusses feedback and evaluation in more detail.

Decision Making

In many of our former curriculum planning endeavors we have not developed clear ideas about who needs to be involved in curriculum development decision making. Generally, we have left the decision making to the experts, the major problem being the dissemination of decisions to those who will carry them out. The approach suggested here is that curriculum development in a teacher education program can be productive only if all those likely to be affected by the curriculum are parties to, or represented in, its development and its evaluation. In curriculum development the first question is not, "Who knows?" but, "Who is most directly affected?" The second question is, "Who is likely to have some relationship to its operation?" Consequently, the decision-making apparatus should involve students in the program, teachers in schools, college or university faculty, school and university administrators, children who will be affected by the teachers coming from the program, and adult community representatives who will be affected by the program. As the program is developed, it may become necessary to involve personnel from state departments of education, representatives from teachers' unions, and perhaps even the funding sources for curriculum development: legislators, boards of education, and trustees. Earlier in this paper we made some tentative designations of who might be involved in the curriculum-instruction design process.

As the reader has seen in the example provided in chapter 2, the model for decision making within a systems approach is applicable to decision making within the curriculum design process. The model applies within each of the seven steps in the curriculum-instruction design process.

Instructional Modules

No attempt has been made in this chapter to prescribe the way a teacher education curriculum should be structured, that is, how the selected objectives should be organized. Whether this organization is along subject matter lines, interdisciplinary lines, or some other approach is a decision that must be made in each program. However, as was mentioned in chapter 1, the authors of this volume argue strongly for the use of instructional modules as the basic organizing unit. Briefly, an instructional module consists of an objective or set of related objectives, a rationale describing the importance of these objectives for prospective teachers, learning alternatives designed to help the student achieve and demonstrate the objectives, and preassessment and postassessment procedures designed to determine the student's level of mastery relevant to the objectives.

The rationale for using the module as the basic organizing unit is strong.

1. Because they are objective oriented, modules are consistent with the systems approach.

2. Because of their objective orientation, modules can be evaluated much more easily than semester-long courses.

3. Modules are much more easily added, changed, or discarded than courses.

4. Because modules usually do not run a full semester (they usually vary from a day to several weeks), a more flexible use can be made of instructional personnel and student time.

5. More options are available to the students in the sequencing and composition of their curriculum.

6. Module credit—a fraction of a semester credit hour—can be assigned to each module and easily converted to the semester credit system for record-keeping purposes.

If a curriculum is designed with the instructional module as the basic organizing unit, care must be taken to integrate the individual modules. In other words, the modules must be so built from a carefully conceptualized framework as to insure a synthesis of learning experiences. The student must not feel he is jumping a series of unconnected hurdles. Instead, he should be able to perceive each module as part of a total program.

Footnotes

1. Kathryn V. Feyereisen, A. John Fiorino, Arlene T. Nowak, "A Systems Approach to Curriculum Design—A New Rationale," in *Supervision and Curriculum Renewal: A Systems Approach* (New York: Appleton-Century-Crofts, 1970), pp. 130–50.

2. An excellent model for problem identification and program planning has been described by Andre L. Delbecq & Andy Van de Ven, "A Group Process Model for Problem Identification and Program Planning," *Journal of Applied Behavioral Science* 7, no. 4 (1971): 466–92.

References

Delbecq, Andre L. & Andy Ven de Ven, "A Group Process Model for Problem Identification and Program Planning." *Journal of Applied Behavioral Science* 7: 466–92.

Feyereisen, Kathryn V., A John Fiorino & Arlene R. Nowak. *Supervision and Curriculum Renewal: A Systems Approach.* New York: Appleton-Century-Crofts, 1970.

Haubrick, Vernon F., ed. *Freedom, Bureaucracy and Schooling.* Washington, D.C.: Assoc. for Supervision and Curriculum Development, 1971.

Joyce, Bruce & Marsha Weil, eds. *Perspectives for Reform in Teacher Education.* Englewood Cliffs, N.J.: Prentice-Hall, 1972.

McClure, Robert M., ed. *The Curriculum Retrospect and Prospect: Seventieth Yearbook of the National Society for the Study of Education, Part 1.* Chicago: NSSE, 1971.

Runkel, Philip, Roger Harrison & Margaret Runkel, eds. *The Changing College Classroom.* San Francisco: Jossey-Bass, 1969.

Smith, B. O., ed. *Research in Teacher Education: A Symposium for the American Educational Research Association.* Englewood Cliffs, N.J.: Prentice-Hall, 1971.

Wilson, L. Craig. *The Open Access Curriculum.* Boston: Allyn & Bacon, 1971.

4
Specifying Assumptions, Goals, and Objectives

Charles E. Johnson
Gilbert F. Shearron

Chapter Objectives

The reader will be able to describe the process of specifying (1) program assumptions, (2) program goals, and (3) program objectives in a competency based teacher education program.

Introduction

If we think of a teacher education program as an instructional system designed to achieve certain purposes, it is necessary to determine what those purposes are. In systems terminology, what is the expected output of the program? In most instances, the main purpose of a teacher education program is to produce teachers who possess certain knowledge; appropriate attitudes toward themselves and their peers and students; performance skills; and the ability to put these all together to bring about desirable learning, attitudes, and behavior in their pupils. It is unlikely that many teacher educators would disagree with the above statement. However, a number of questions must still be asked, such as: What knowledge, attitudes, and skills should the prospective teacher possess? And what changes do we wish to bring about in children?

The answers to these questions, as well as the means and the different human resources and styles used to achieve the goals derived from the answers, largely determine the differences among teacher education programs. To determine the output of the system, i.e., the kinds of teachers the program wishes to produce, it is necessary to develop a set of assumptions about teaching from which can be generated statements of goals. From these goals we can generate more specific objectives that define the competencies a teacher will need in order to achieve the goals of the program.

Programs that have different basic assumptions about the role of the teacher will certainly function in different ways and will produce teachers who operate in different ways. Most teacher education programs today have not developed sets of assumptions about teaching. Consequently, they cannot conceptualize clearly the role of the teacher. Until this is done, there will be no precise understanding of what kinds of teachers are to be produced, nor will it be possible to determine the extent of internal consistency among the assumptions, goals, and objectives. If this internal consistency does not exist, the program will be schizophrenic in nature and may produce conflicting messages to all involved in the program.

The need is clear. Teacher education programs must be based on a conceptualization of the roles of the teacher. Any program that operates without a strong theoretical or empirical base lacks purposeful direction. This chapter will attempt to describe what teaching assumptions, goals, and objectives look like, their importance to the overall success of the program, and the procedures for developing them.

Specifying Assumptions

Assumptions about teaching are beliefs that are fundamental to the conceptualized role of the teacher. As such, they differ from assumptions about how the teacher education program should be organized. While this chapter is primarily concerned with assumptions about teaching, assumptions about how the teacher education program should be organized (e.g., teacher education programs should be systematic and capable of regeneration) should also be specified by program developers. Assumptions about teaching are based on what we believe about how the human organism develops and learns, society's present and future needs, and the role of the teacher in the instructional process. Modifications or changes in these assumptions usually suggest modifications or changes in the teacher education program.

Assumptions here are regarded as hypotheses that are expressions of values. They are thought to be valid but may or may not have been demonstrated. Thus, assumptions are statements of what is thought to be effective, right, good, or desirable. Some illustrations of teaching assumptions are:

1. Teachers model their teaching on selected teaching practices they have experienced.

2. Teachers must have knowledge about how environments affect people in order to relate to the needs satisfaction of pupils.

3. In order for a teacher to meet the needs of individual pupils he must possess a wide variety of teaching competencies.

4. Learning is more apt to occur when the learner possesses a sense of identity (who he is), a sense of power (control over himself and his environment), and a sense of connectedness (his relationships with others).

5. Each person is unique in the way he learns most effectively.

To understand the importance of assumptions in program development, suppose one assumes that each child is unique in the way he learns most effectively. Then the teacher education program must prepare teachers who can make provisions for individual learning styles, and who themselves have been able to use their own learning styles in the teacher preparation program. Schools are then developed that allow the pupil to choose, with counseling, alternatives best suited to his learning style. For example, if a pupil has difficulty with verbal learning, then, if possible, nonverbal learning alternatives are made available to him. On the other hand, if one assumes there are no differences in learning styles, a program is developed that requires everyone to learn in the same way. Each pupil reads the same materials, listens to the same lectures, views the same visuals, and is expected to respond the same to test items.

Thus, the assumptions one makes tend to provide direction for the total teacher education program. They suggest the conceptual framework of the program; how the curriculum-instruction subsystem will operate; the relationship of the training institutions to other agencies, such as the public schools; the organization and management of the program; and the relationships between all the individuals involved in the program. Therefore, the program's basic assumptions about teaching must be made explicit for all involved in the program. In systems terms, the purposes of the program, which are derived from the assumptions, dictate the processes and components of the program.

Specifying Goals and Objectives

The previous section has shown how assumptions about teaching are generalized statements that provide the value system on which the program is founded. It should be noted, however, that these values do not specify what a teacher should know, feel, or be able to do. For this information one must turn to goals and objectives. Teacher education goals are statements explaining the mission of the teacher education program. That is, they tell in general terms what the trainees of the program are to accomplish. These statements, when reduced to the more specific terms called instructional objectives, indicate the competencies that teachers must possess if they are to effect desirable changes in pupil behavior.

Goals for Teacher Education

In the past, goals for teacher education have usually been statements that indicated concern for professional education and broad liberal education. Little has been written that clearly defines comprehensive goals for teacher education. Nonetheless, teacher education goals, whether implicit or explicit, are one basis for developing and specifying competencies. The goals statements should be broad and inclusive but not so broad as to allow a variety of interpretation. The authors believe that there are many sources for determining the goals for teacher education programs but that the main sources are assumptions about teaching and the needs of the society the program is to serve, particularly as expressed by those individuals most directly involved in the program. That is, the goals of any teacher education program should not only reflect what we know to be effective teaching, but also parallel the beliefs of society about what education should accomplish.

Societal beliefs about the function of education have usually reflected the dominant sociological and psychological concepts of the time they were identified. These goals are broadly based, far-reaching, and often abstract. They have their origin in the society's aspirations, values, realities, philosophical orientations, and historical referents. They are often expressed by governing boards, state legislators, professional organizations, and union officials. Some social beliefs that might be considered determinants for the goals of a teacher education program are:

1. Education should provide persons with the ability to think rationally and the desire to exercise this ability.

2. Education should prepare individuals to become contributing members of their society.

3. Education should provide for the development of attitudes and values that lead to a racially integrated society.

Beliefs such as these are the beginning point if one believes that schools should be responsive to the needs of the society they serve.

Goals for teacher education that might be derived from the above social determinants are expressed in the following statement:

A teacher education program will provide teachers with the knowledge and skills with which to guide children in acquiring behaviors that will allow them to (1) think rationally and possess the desire to exercise this capability; (2) become contributing members of their society; and (3) develop attitudes and values that lead to a racially integrated society.

The following are illustrations of other possible goals for teacher education. Note that whereas some seem to be related to empirical assumptions about teaching, others seem more closely related to social determinants, and still others seem to relate to what is thought to be knowledge about man and how he learns.

1. A teacher education program will help each teacher develop a personally relevant teaching style.

2. A teacher education program will prepare each teacher to employ teaching behaviors that will assist each pupil to acquire a positive attitude toward school and the learning process.

3. A teacher education program will prepare teachers to help children acquire understanding of their social and physical environment and means by which it may be modified and/or changed to meet the needs of man and society.

4. A teacher education program will provide for the preparation of teachers who can help children acquire an appreciation of the social and physical environment that surrounds them.

5. A teacher education program will help teachers acquire a sound understanding of how the human organism learns to adjust to and control his social and physical environment and how children and youth best acquire the behaviors that will assist them in exercising the processes of adjustment and control.

During the process of specifying goals for teacher education, it is imperative to maintain a consistent viewpoint. That is to say, the desired effect of the implementation of one goal should not conflict with the desired effect of another. Furthermore, program goals must be consistent with program assumptions.

Figure 1 graphically depicts the relationships of the activities recommended in this chapter for specifying the goals of a teacher education program. The two squares at the top of the figure indicate that the initial activities include specifying assumptions about teaching and assessing social determinants. Once these are available, a

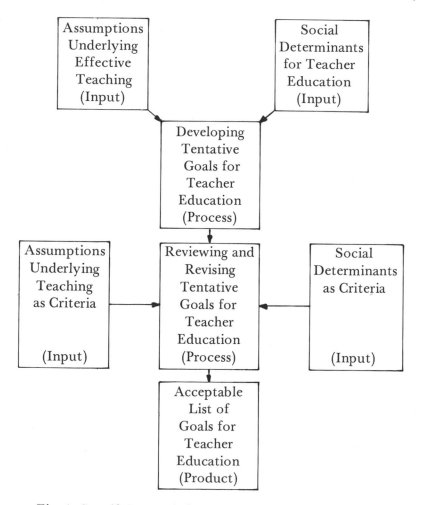

Fig. 1. Specifying goals for a teacher education program

tentative list of goals for the teacher education program is developed. This tentative list of goals is then reviewed and revised for consistency, using the teaching assumptions and social determinants as criteria. Finally, a consistent list of goals for teacher education evolves to serve as the foundation for determining the specific nature for the output of the program.

Objectives for Teacher Education

The instructional, or teaching, objectives for a teacher education program are statements of the competencies thought to be essential for effective teaching. They are derived from the goals for teacher education but are much more specific. For each identified teacher education program goal there are usually several instructional objectives that describe competencies to be demonstrated by the prospective teacher. The term *competencies* was defined in chapter 1 as the "attitudes, understandings, skills and behaviors that facilitate intellectual, social, emotional, and physical growth in children." The authors have chosen to use the terms *competency* and *objective* synonymously in this volume. It should be noted, however, that objectives may be stated at various levels of specificity. The authors believe that statements of teacher competencies should indicate the expected teacher behavior, but should be stated somewhat generally. These competencies may in turn be stated more specifically to provide direction for instructional development and evaluation.

Figure 2 graphically depicts the relationship between goals and objectives. For each of the goals of teacher education, a number of teacher competencies may be specified, each reflective of the goal from which it is derived.

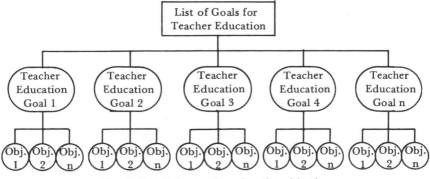

Fig. 2. Specifying teacher education objectives

The following are teacher competencies that might systematically be derived from a specified list of program goals. Note that some are applicable to the teaching of particular school subjects; others relate generally to what might be called "the teaching process"; and still others concern themselves with the learner's self-realization.

1. The teacher demonstrates an understanding of word recognition skills and the ability to teach them effectively.

2. The teacher diagnoses pupil study performance and prescribes and implements procedures for assisting learners to apply effective work study skills.

3. The teacher evaluates pupil development in musical performance using acceptable judgmental criteria.

4. The teacher uses evaluation feedback to assess his teaching behavior and amends his behavior accordingly.

5. The teacher engages learners in discussions of contemporary social problems during which the learners identify their values and indicate how these values affect their proposed solutions to these problems.

6. The teacher adapts, modifies, and combines various communications media to develop effective instructional materials designed to satisfy specific teaching objectives.

7. The teacher creates a classroom atmosphere conducive to personal acceptance and comfortable interaction for all participants in the learning environment.

8. The teacher guides learners in acquiring oral communication skills that allow them to convey with considered intent such elements as meaning, mood, emotion, overtones, and variety.

9. The teacher effectively evaluates the products of the learner's written language using acceptable criteria.

10. The teacher uses classroom management procedures that organize and coordinate the cooperative efforts of students in ways that lead to the accomplishment of individual and educational objectives.

Most of these statements of teacher competencies can be reduced to even more specific instructional objectives. For example, the following statement of objectives might be drawn from competency 10 above. Note that these five objectives are at the consequence level rather than the knowledge of performance level: a distinction made in the introduction of this book.

In a classroom setting, the teacher will:

1. Achieve group cohesiveness, pride, morale, and cooperation
2. Establish and maintain productive and effective group norms
3. Improve group effectiveness using participatory problem-solving techniques
4. Change inappropriate and unproductive patterns of behavior
5. Handle group conflict in nonpunitive ways

Specification Procedures

The process of developing assumptions, goals, and objectives for a competency based teacher education program is complex and difficult. In simplest terms, these processes involve collection of large amounts of information and considerable discussion by many persons with different backgrounds, expertise, and values. In such a situation, consensus is difficult to achieve.

The authors suggest that these processes be viewed as consisting of two major phases: (1) designing a plan for specifying program assumptions, goals, and objectives; and (2) implementing and operating the plan.

How specifically and in what detail the objectives should be stated are questions that every curriculum developer must ultimately answer. Objectives can include such details as the behavior expected, the conditions under which the behavior will be performed, and the degree to which the behavior will be demonstrated. For example, an objective might be: "The teacher education student will ask a minimum of five probing questions in a five-minute microteaching lesson with a group of four fifth-grade students."

While this type of objective has the advantage of great specificity, it also has the disadvantages of convergence and restrictiveness. The real intent of this objective is to ensure that the teacher education student will be able to ask probing questions of school age children. While this skill might be demonstrated under the stated conditions and criterion level, it might also be demonstrated under other conditions and different criterion levels. The objective might better be worded: "The teacher education student will demonstrate the ability to ask probing questions of school age children." Whoever is to evaluate this objective must then ask himself what is acceptable evidence that this objective has been achieved. We do not believe it is advisable to specify *a priori* the conditions and criterion level for demonstrating competency. It seems to us that individualization can occur only when the student and instructor negotiate these factors.[1]

As was mentioned in chapter 1, the objectives developed should not be limited to the cognitive or knowledge domain but should include statements of competencies to be acquired that reflect performance and consequence outcomes. In fact, we contend that one of the most favorable characteristics of a competency based teacher education program is that it places greater emphasis on performance and consequence competencies than traditional programs.

Designing a Plan

The initial activities in designing a plan are normally carried out by concerned persons who have assumed or been given the responsibility for effecting program change. The product of their efforts is a preliminary report justifying the need for program change and conveying to others yet to be involved the purpose, complexity, and seriousness of the proposed undertaking. The activities included in this initial thrust have already been suggested in the general management design offered in chapter 2. Applied to the present task, these activities include making a study of the present program; determining how assumptions, goals, and objectives should be used in program development; making a preliminary search for existing statements of assumptions, goals, and objectives; and evaluating existing program development strategies.

When the initiators are satisfied with the preliminary plan, it should be submitted to a decision-making body as suggested in chapter 2. The decision makers might first receive orientation to the preliminary plan. Next they could examine the proposed activities contained in the preliminary plan, looking for errors, omissions, and unreasonable estimates and verifying the suitability of the recommended specialists, consultants, and other participants. In general, they would try to obtain a consensus among themselves about which operational plan or strategy would provide the desired statement. It should be pointed out that this could result in a complete restructuring of the initial plan. This is not likely, however; if the preliminary plan was carefully designed, it is more likely that the types of changes recommended would be modifications of certain activities, sequences, time schedules, and personnel lists.

Implementation of the Plan

If there are enough members on the working team, they may choose to form two groups and simultaneously pursue the activities associated with determining the assumptions about teaching and those associated with identifying the social determinants of the teacher education program.

If they follow the suggested plan in Chapter 2, the group that has the responsibility of creating the statements of assumptions about teaching will first identify those persons other than themselves who will ultimately be responsible for choosing the appropriate assumptions. They will collect information or data on assumptions about effective teaching by using library resources, consulting with specialists, and conferring with each other. As a result of these investigations, they might choose to produce working papers containing summary lists. One set of papers might contain lists of assumptions about how particular subjects, such as reading, science, or music, should be taught. Another set might focus on the ways in which our knowledge about the human organism and how it learns should affect instruction. Still another might focus on what are regarded as effective behaviors for teaching certain attitudes and values. Once the investigators have reached consensus and produced an initial set of statements, these papers are set aside and regarded as tentative until they are reviewed—along with other pertinent information—by those responsible for final decisions.

The task of specifying social determinants for teacher education is tedious and costly in terms of time and effort if the working team intends to produce an original statement. Since much has been done in this area, suitable lists might justifiably be obtained by search and review of existing materials. If, however, it is considered essential to develop original statements of social determinants, the team should begin in the same manner as the group specifying the assumptions about teaching. The authors believe that while professional workers should establish the assumptions underlying effective teaching, both laymen and professionals should be involved in identifying social determinants. This is based on the principle that all individuals and social groups concerned or affected by the education of children and youth should be represented when the educational goals of their society are determined. Adherence to this principle requires so careful a selection of the persons to serve that no group is denied representation.[2]

We suggest that the group might save time and effort by having the professional members of the group make a preliminary study. They might use literature review, consultation, and conferences to produce working papers, as did the group specifying assumptions about teaching. In this case, however, the papers would have to be in fairly nontechnical language that could be understood by laymen. One paper might summarize authoritative information about man and society; another might list what have been found to be acceptable goals for education; and still another might concern itself with the present and predicted capabilities of professional education. A series of meetings over a period of several weeks might be a suitable arrangement for bringing the investigating forces together to produce a preliminary list of statements describing social determinants.

When the lists of assumptions and social determinants are completed, the team may then turn to specifying the goals for teacher education. Using the tentative lists, the team states the goals for teacher education one by one. Next the team must review and revise these goals, using the tentative lists of assumptions and determinants as criteria and continually checking for consistency and compatibility among the various elements. Having completed this preliminary work, the team then submits the results to the body of decision makers delegated to accept, reject, and/or revise the various statements.

After agreement has been reached regarding the goals for the curriculum-instruction subsystem, it is time to specify the instructional objectives for the program. The recommended process is approximately the same as that for determining the assumptions about teaching and should also be undertaken by professional workers. However, there is one important difference. For each established goal, there are numerous program objectives; because these objectives are more specifically related to breakdown categories of human activities and academic disciplines, we suggest that several small working groups be created. Each might be assigned either one specific goal or a few related ones from which to draw instructional objectives.

While the instructional objectives are being reviewed and revised, the team should examine an operational consideration not previously evident: that is, the possibility of omissions. The authors recognize that there may be sources other than goals for teacher education that could be valuable in determining instructional objectives. Some objectives may be too subtle if only the goals are considered as sources. Other sources might include observations of teachers on the job, the school's objectives for children and youth, and principles of classroom organization and management. Thus, before the lists of objectives are considered complete, the team may choose to make a thorough search for any that may have been overlooked.

As a final step, a small group of professional workers should summarize and assemble all the ideas produced in a single document that expresses the considered educational viewpoint of all the participants. Some of the more essential parts of such a document might be: (a) a statement of purpose, (b) a rationale, (c) a list of assumptions underlying effective teaching, (d) a list of social determinants, and (e) a classified list of program goals and instructional objectives. When reproduced and distributed, this document would be a constant reference for the competency based teacher education program being designed.

Summary

This chapter has attempted to provide the reader with an introduction to the assumptions, goals, and objectives for a curriculum-instruction subsystem and the procedures by which they may be specified. The authors point out in closing that the procedures suggested in this chapter are only one approach; there are others. Our purpose has been to provide the reader with ideas that may be adapted to help program planners systematically accomplish the first logical step in developing a competency based teacher education program: the specification of assumptions, goals, and objectives.

Footnotes

1. See Norman E. Gronlund, *Stating Behavioral Objectives for Classroom Instruction* (New York: Macmillan, 1970), pp. 4-5.
2. We think it wise at this point to remind the reader that the processes

described in this chapter refer specifically to the curriculum-instruction sub-system and not to other subsystems within the total program. While it is appropriate and necessary to involve clients of the teacher education program in the determination of the curriculum-instruction subsystem's goals, the goals and objectives of other subsystems, such as the information subsystem, may be so specialized as to nullify the value of client involvement in their specification.

References

Block, James H., ed. *Mastery Learning: Theory and Practice.* New York: Holt, Rinehart & Winston, 1971.

Bloom, Benjamin S. et al. *Taxonomy of Educational Objectives: Handbook 1, The Cognitive Domain.* New York: David McKay Co., 1956.

Educational Policies Commission. *The Central Purpose of American Education.* Washington: National Education Assoc., 1961.

Joyce, Bruce R. & Berj Harootunian. *The Structure of Teaching.* Chicago: Science Research Associates, 1967.

Kearney, Nolan C. *Elementary School Objectives.* New York: Russell Sage Foundation, 1953.

Mager, Robert F. *Preparing Instructional Objectives.* Palo Alto, Calif.: Fearon, 1962.

McAshan, H. H. *Writing Behavioral Objectives.* New York: Harper & Row, 1970.

Plan for Evaluating the Quality of Education Programs in Pennsylvania. Princeton, N.J.: Educational Testing Service, 1965.

Popham, J. W. & E. L. Baker. *Establishing Instructional Goals.* Englewood Cliffs, N.J.: Prentice-Hall, 1970.

Popham, J. W. et al. *Instructional Objectives.* AREA Monograph Series on Curriculum Evaluation. Elliott W. Eisner, "Instructional and Expressive Educational Objectives: Their Formulation and Use in Curriculum." Chicago: Rand McNally, 1969.

Tyler, R. W. *Basic Principles of Curriculum and Instruction.* Chicago: University of Chicago Press, 1950.

5
Developing Instructional Strategies

Wilford A. Weber

Charles Rathbone

Chapter Objectives

The reader will be able to explain the process of: (1) describing an instructional philosophy; (2) selecting instructional strategies; (3) selecting and constructing instructional materials, equipment, and facilities; and (4) selecting, training, and orienting instructional personnel in a competency based teacher education program.

Introduction

Unfortunately, the task of instituting curricular change in a teacher education program is often characterized as a search for answers to the following question: How can the personnel, materials, equipment, and facilities of the present program be employed in the implementation of the new program? The problems implied by that question serve as constraints in the process of designing and implementing new programs. Because of these constraints, the results are too often patchworks of ill-fitting compromises. Some excuse this piecemeal approach by claiming that other approaches are not possible because of financial constraints. They cite as evidence situations in which external funds have stimulated the change process only as long as those funds were available and initial spurts of innovative activities found little institutional commitment when outside funds were withdrawn. While it must be granted that financial considerations are a very serious limitation, poor planning seems to be the greater villain: a villain not easily dismissed.

The importance of good planning cannot be overstressed. Good planning should approach the problem of curricular change through an examination of the question of programmatic goals while temporarily ignoring a consideration of current personnel, materials, equipment, and facilities. Perhaps the initial question faced should be: What specific competencies should program graduates have and use to facilitate growth in children? The process of answering this question forces program designers to be honest in their design of instructional activities. A search for task relevance, that is, a continued appreciation of what instructional program designers should be about, is made far less confusing by a clear awareness of the competencies desired of program graduates. The goal statements resulting from such an appreciation may appear quite similar to the goals stated in more traditional teacher education programs, yet the processes of instruction and the component activities of the processes will generally be quite different. This seems to be a most important point: perhaps it is not only that the goals of teacher education must be changed; the processes of achieving those goals— the instruction—must also change.

Keeping those program objectives in mind helps designers relate processes with products; that is, they can see which processes of instruction will promote specified competencies in program graduates. A related issue is that even where programs have clearly defined the competencies students should acquire—and such programs have been rare—they have not specified the assumptions underlying the philosophy of instruction intended to facilitate the student's achievement of those competencies.

The process of describing the assumptions underlying the instructional philosophy of a program is the first step in the design of the instructional strategies and activities of that program. This chapter first deals with processes of describing assumptions basic to the program as they provide a rationale for instructional program decisions. This is followed by consideration of: (1) the process of selecting strategies; (2) the process of selecting and/or constructing instructional materials, equipment, and facilities appropriate to specific objectives and competencies and an instructional philosophy;

and (3) the role, selection, and training of instructional personnel.

The Process of Describing the Instructional Philosophy

Chapter 4 has already discussed the processes of program goal generation and the development of program objectives; the position taken in this chapter is that instructional philosophy, strategies, and activities are, and must be, a direct outgrowth of program goals and objectives. Experience suggests that careful attention to the explication of the instructional philosophy of a program generates a large number of assumptions. With the recognition that the specification of a wide range of assumptions of both a general nature and a situation specific nature is not only possible but necessary, there are four key assumptions. To be effective, a teacher education program should (1) be competency based, (2) be regenerative, (3) be personalized and consumer oriented, and (4) provide good models of instruction.

Competency Based Teacher Education Programs

The notion of competency based teacher education has been a major focus of this volume. As defined earlier, a competency based teacher education program specifies the competencies to be acquired by the student and the criteria to be applied in assessing his competency and holds the student accountable for meeting those criteria. Those competencies are the attitudes, understandings, skills, and behaviors that facilitate intellectual, social, emotional, and physical growth in children. Three kinds of criteria are used in assessing the student's competency: (1) knowledge criteria for the student's cognitive understandings; (2) performance criteria for his teaching behaviors; and (3) product criteria, which assess his teaching effectiveness by examining the achievements of his pupils. Competency based programs emphasize the use of performance and product criteria, while traditional programs have emphasized knowledge criteria.

Some of the characteristics that differentiate competency based programs from traditional programs play a major role in influencing the nature of instructional processes:

1. In a competency based program, criteria for achievement of the objectives are held constant and time varies, while in a traditional program, time is held constant and achievement varies.

2. Competency based programs emphasize exit requirements,

while traditional programs place heavy emphasis on entrance requirements.

3. Competency based programs tend to be more field-oriented than traditional programs; consequently, students spend a great deal of time in the public schools in interaction with children and many of their competencies are evaluated in that setting. In traditional programs instructional activities and assessment, except for the student-teaching experience, usually take place in the college classroom.

4. In competency based programs clearly stated objectives are used to specify the competencies to be acquired by the student.

Regenerative Teacher Education Programs

Teacher education programs must reflect the changing nature of society and the effect this change process has on the role of the teacher. To be most effective, teachers need to be critically, but openly, receptive to change. If they are to help students acquire such attitudes, teacher education programs must be open and flexible. The basic implication is that one cannot educate teachers in the same way one processes computer cards and expect them to become self-reliant, self-renewing, self-directed individuals capable of critically examining themselves as people and teachers.

As noted earlier, the systems analysis approach is in part an attempt to make and keep programs relevant through rigorous application of systemic techniques in program design and management. The continuous, careful examination of the performance and effectiveness of program graduates through the use of feedback allows for data based decision making regarding the selection of students, the allocation of resources, and the modification of instruction. Thus, the program becomes regenerative, an open system that welcomes and accommodates change.

Personalized Teacher Education Programs

The assumption that instructional aspects of the teacher education program must be designed to meet the unique needs of each student places at least three major demands on program designers:

1. A given instructional objective or activity must be appropriate to the interests, abilities, and learning styles of the student.

2. Procedures for diagnosing individual needs must be designed to permit the student to develop a realistic self-awareness so that he can design his personal program.

3. Feedback systems must monitor the progress of each student and the effectiveness of the program so that information is continually available to both students and program designers.

In short, the instructional activities of the program must be personalized for the student. This statement becomes an assumption underlying the design and implementation of all instructional activities.

Personalization of instruction is the second keystone of the instructional philosophy, the first being competency based concepts. In order to personalize instruction, it seems most beneficial for the designer to consider instructional modules providing for self-pacing and alternate routes, student involvement in the decision-making processes, use of new technology, and interdisciplinary approaches.

The Instructional Module

In its simplest terms, an instructional module is a series of learning activities that facilitate the student's achievement and demonstration of a specific objective or set of objectives. As viewed here, an instructional module is characterized by:

a. A rationale serving two purposes: (1) to describe the purpose and importance of the objectives of the module in empirical, theoretical, and/or practical terms; and (2) to place the module and the objectives of the module within the context of the total program

b. An objective or set of objectives that specify the competency or competencies the student is expected to demonstrate

c. A description of prerequisites to the module, if any

d. Pre-assessment procedures—usually diagnostic in nature—that allow the student to demonstrate mastery of the objective or objectives and to "test out"

e. Learning alternatives—various instructional options available to the student—that contribute to the student's achievement of the objective or objectives

f. Postassessment procedures that allow the student to demonstrate achievement of the objective or objectives of the module

g. Remedial procedures for those students who are unable to demonstrate achievement of the objective or objectives on the post-assessment

The use of instructional modules increases the possibilities for alternative means of instruction, the individualization and personalization of instruction, and self-pacing within a module and the total program sequence. The module approach also makes it easier to change the program. As the competencies required of the student change, modules can be added, modified, or deleted with less effort than it usually takes to change a course. Modules, it should be noted, may require varying lengths of student time depending on the objectives and the pace at which a student works.

This discussion of the instructional module has touched only briefly on the notions of self-pacing and alternative routes. Before leaving this section of the chapter, perhaps it would be wise to elaborate on these two concepts:

1. Self-pacing. If instruction is to be personalized, the length of time a student spends in any one module and in the program should be a function of his unique learning style and his capacity and willingness to master the specified competency or competencies. Self-pacing ensures that the student will be able to acquire competencies relevant to the objectives of each module and of the program at his own rate of learning.

2. Alternative routes. The concept of alternative routes within a module or through a series of modules arises from the realization that an inflexible sequence of instructional activities may not be the most effective way for a student to learn. For example, one student may learn the skill of asking divergent questions most effectively by microteaching, while another may best acquire that skill by working with self-instructional materials, and yet another may practice with a class of children in a school setting. Therefore, to personalize a program in a meaningful fashion, program designers must provide alternative routes to each objective. Indeed, the student should be encouraged to design his own route. To do so, the student must have access to a wide range of resources and experiences.

Just as there should be alternative routes of instruction within the modules, there should be alternative routes through the entire program. That is, the student must be able to build his own program by choosing and sequencing his experiences to fit his needs. This will require program designers to limit prerequisites to a bare minimum.

Student Involvement in the Decision-Making Process

A central aspect of program personalization is the provision for student participation in the design of his instructional program and experiences. Clearly, teacher educators must be consumer oriented, and they must not see themselves as being responsible for all decisions, even if they are "acting in the best interests of their students." Students must be responsible for their own learning if they are to be held accountable.

Campus unrest suggests that we have no alternative but to involve students as never before. As teacher educators, our primary role may be to design procedures that provide students with information permitting data based decisions. Consequently, programs must provide instruction relevant to the needs articulated by students. In other words, students must have the right to formulate objectives in addition to those stipulated by the program, and instruction must be provided to help students meet those self-determined objectives.

A related facet of this issue is the notion that teacher education programs should allow each student to specialize in a particular area, such as grade level or content. The program should encourage students to select areas of specialization compatible with their interests and abilities. It must also provide instruction that will help the student develop the competencies relevant to his chosen area of specialization.

Use of New Technology

The effective teacher education program must use a full range of innovative materials, equipment, and facilities to foster student progress. The program must combine the best of humanistic and scientific approaches. The new technology must free faculty to spend more time in one-to-one and small group settings as their responsibility to impart knowledge decreases. The new technology must be used to make learning more efficient, and it must expand the student's environment and time. But it must not become the student's master. Appropriately used, the new technology can increase the possibilities for personalization of the instructional program; badly used, it can make the instructional process impersonal and mechanistic. As was emphasized in chapter 2, first the purposes or goals must be made clear, then the appropriate components can be chosen to help achieve the objectives.

Interdisciplinary Approaches

An interdisciplinary approach to teacher education provides the student with a wide range of experiences, which are nonetheless integrated and focused on a particular set of objectives. Reality based objectives are less likely to stem from a single discipline area than from a variety of disciplines. Interdisciplinary approaches should decrease program fragmentation and curricular overlaps or gaps. In addition, the interdisciplinary approach that is consciously pluralistic will broaden thé teacher's repertoire while providing a basis for indepth specialization.

The Process of Selecting Instructional Strategies

After examining this set of underlying assumptions about the instructional philosophy of a teacher education program and establishing the program's objectives, the next step is to select appropriate instructional strategies for achieving the instructional objectives. Clearly, these strategies must be consistent with the program's conceptualized philosophy.

Our space is too limited for even a brief description of all the various strategies appropriate to the assumptions stated earlier. Therefore, we shall concentrate on a few strategies that represent the more recent innovations. Each of these is compatible with the philosophical assumptions stated earlier, and the linkage between strategy and assumption is briefly noted.

Microteaching

The advent of relatively inexpensive videotape recorders has made microteaching a practical learning technique. Fundamentally, the procedure involves having the student practice a specific teaching behavior—such as praising students, using nonverbal cues, or asking higher-order questions—before a small group of students or role-playing peers for a relatively short period of time. The practice session is videotaped. The student views the tape, perhaps with a faculty member, and notes the congruence or incongruence between the intended behavior and the observed behavior. Generally, the student then reteaches the lesson with a new group of students or peers, focusing on the development of the same skill. The student again views his performance, noting his practiced skill. The instant-replay capability of videotape allows a measure of practice under conditions seldom attained in teacher education. The student can practice in a situation that diminishes the overwhelming number of variables often faced in a regular classroom setting and can concentrate his efforts on developing one skill with a minimum of extraneous interference.

Microteaching is clearly compatible with the notion of competency based teacher education and its emphasis on the assessment of competencies through the use of performance criteria. It also reflects the concern of competency based programs with reality orientation. Moreover, it is one use of the new technology that clearly personalizes the student's experiences.

Simulation

Persons concerned with designing instructional strategies should become familiar with the notions of simulation. In the simplest terms, simulations are role-playing experiences that place the student in a reality based problem situation but protect him from the potential consequences of an actual experience. For example, a group of students may play elected school board members who are faced with a 10 percent budget reduction and must set spending priorities for their school district. The students would gain understanding of the nature of educational priorities and the processes of a school board and a host of other cognitive and affective by-products without suffering the consequences of an actual situation.

Simulations differ greatly regarding their objectives, content, duration, and mode. Many simulations are open-ended and affectively oriented. Some are brief, lasting only an hour, for example; others go on for days. Most simulations make use of media; many are self-instructional.

Simulations are compatible with the notions of competency based teacher education in that they provide a reality oriented approach to learning. Moreover, their conscious effort to protect the student represents a genuine recognition of the worth of the individual. The fact that most simulations make use of media reflects an appropriate use of the new technology.

Computer Assisted Instruction

Effective personalization of instruction requires the collection and use of performance assessment data about each student as he works through each of the program modules. Such feedback systems are an important part of making and keeping the program regenerative. In addition to this very important record-keeping function, the

immediate feedback capability of the computer increases the effectiveness of certain types of independent learning activities. For
example, even a module in which the evaluation takes the form of an
objective, written test can require a great deal of data-processing
work. However, a properly programed computer terminal can give
the student immediate feedback about his test results, compile a
continuous master progress chart for the student, and provide data
on the progress of other students through a given module. The man-
hours presently spent on these tasks suggest a great need for com-
puterized instructional feedback systems.

The computer can also be used for direct instruction. Through
the use of branching programs, computer assisted instruction is becoming a viable way to facilitate the learning of students. Individuals
concerned with the selection of instructional methodologies, however, will find that present computer assisted instruction costs are
rather high. Indeed, costs are often prohibitive. We feel that in the
future costs will decrease to a level where cost-benefit ratios are
favorable.

When one thinks of computers, there is an easy association with
the new technology. Obviously, computer assisted instruction—and
we include the use of feedback data to make individual student and
program decisions—is a good example of the use of the new technology. It is an appropriate use, because the services provided help to
personalize the student's experience.

Programed Instruction

Competency based programs specify many skills that can be
learned in small, sequential steps. For example, a reasonable objective might be to recognize and discriminate between statements of
educational objectives by observing and measuring certain pupil behaviors. In order to acquire this competency, a student might read a
book on cognitive learning and listen to a lecture on discrimination
skills. On the other hand, a program could be written in which some
type of media exposes the student to cognitive learning concepts in
small, measured steps and continually reinforces his progress as he
reacts to examples. Part of the program might be a videotaped
presentation of a pupil in a classroom, and the student's task would
be to analyze the pupil's cognitive behaviors. The programed approach enables a somewhat complex objective to be subdivided into

a series of learning steps through which the student can progress at his own rate.

Properly designed programed instruction can have a very positive personalizing effect. Those who would select and design instructional methodologies must recognize that programed instruction may make the student's experiences rigid and uninteresting. They must also see that programed instruction is not confined to the use of programed texts but includes a wide range of media. If the designer can avoid these pitfalls, he will realize the enormous potential of programed instruction. The primary benefit, of course, is the opportunity for independent study and self-pacing.

Interaction Analysis

Interaction analysis techniques provide methods for quantifying and qualifying the teaching process, and they are valuable tools for students to use as they study their own teaching behaviors. Further, they aid the student as he attempts to behave in specific ways. Indeed, when used with microteaching techniques, interaction analysis has been most effective in bringing about teaching behavior changes.

The use of interaction analysis supports the notion of performance assessment by providing objective data about the teaching behaviors specified as competencies to be acquired by the student. It promotes personalization because it allows the student to be more aware of his progress toward achieving those teaching behavior competencies.

Independent Study

The personalization of instruction demands that the student be given opportunities for independent study. This strategy is based on the notion that the student should be responsible for his own learning. In effect this means that the student is left to accomplish a learning task by himself without inputs from either his peers or faculty. Independent learning activities vary widely. They range from one-to-one tutoring in a public school classroom to viewing a slide presentation in a study carrel. They can be brief or lengthy experiences. The common element is that the student works alone, using other resources as he needs them.

Independent study supports both competency based and personalization concepts. The student works at his own pace to acquire specified competencies; he is held accountable for mastering those competencies. Also, independent study clearly allows for self-pacing by the student, thus enhancing the possibilities of personalization.

Human Relations Training

Human relations approaches in teacher education are quite compatible with the philosophy stated earlier. The major benefit of sensitivity training is the student's increased awareness of himself as a person, as a teacher, and as a member of the profession. It seems reasonable to assume that these insights make him more effective both as a teacher and as a learner within the teacher education program.

Sensitivity training and human relations approaches appear to be an essential part of the personalization of instruction. It is imperative that we help an individual cope with his anxieties about teaching, feelings of inadequacy, and self-doubt. An emphasis on cognitive learning to the exclusion of affective needs will produce teachers who cannot cope with their students' affective concerns.

The Process of Selecting and/or Constructing
Instructional Materials, Equipment, and Facilities

This section is not intended to give the reader a complete discussion of the issue of instructional materials, equipment, and facilities. It is our intention simply to alert the teacher education program designer to certain notions not usually explored in the usual treatment of the subject. There are four basic recommendations:

1. The selection and construction of instructional resources must be compatible with the program's instructional philosophy and methodologies. A simple example is the notion that if the program is to be personalized, there must be enough copies of certain books for the student to use those books when he wishes. If the program is to be reality oriented, materials must be continuously updated. Unless the designer fully appreciates the necessity to establish linkages between instructional philosophy, methodologies, and resources, he cannot hope to build an effective program.

2. Instructional resources should be made available to the student from the widest possible range of sources. This notion suggests that one of the benefits of multi-institutional patterns of organiza-

tion is that such patterns broaden the range of material and personnel available to the student. Clearly, a sharing of resources across several institutions is an effective method of decreasing costs; this is particularly important, for example, with regard to the development of instructional materials. To produce a 16mm film for use in a single program may not be economically feasible, but if that cost is shared by a number of programs, the cost per unit is greatly reduced. The wisdom of such arrangements seems clear.

3. Instructional resources must support the program; the program should not be molded by existing or easily obtained resources. The usual piecemeal approach fails to recognize this need; the result is an ill-fitting set of compromises. Teacher educators must either become instructional resource designers or begin to cooperate more closely with instructional technologists if they are to have materials, equipment, and facilities that will increase program effectiveness. Components must be chosen to facilitate the processes which will help achieve program objectives, not vice versa.

4. Teacher education program designers must see that the critical variable in decisions about instructional resources is student time rather than money. Admittedly, money is always an important consideration. But we must begin to achieve a better balance between the present posture, which places financial concerns ahead of human concerns, and one that totally ignores cost factors. It seems inappropriate that a college should spend so much more to educate engineers than teachers, yet per-student costs for teacher education students are usually among the lowest. A major resource within a teacher education program that cannot be obtained in greater quantities is student time. We must stop squandering that resource, even if we must spend more money to do so.

Quite obviously, the teacher education program designer exploring the issues of materials, equipment, and facilities will find a great many questions not raised here. However, if he keeps in mind the four biases described above, he will be well on his way to facing the many problems involved.

The Process of Defining the Roles of and Selecting,
Training, and Orienting Instructional Personnel

Innovative teacher education programs require innovative instructional activities and methodologies. Yet, such activities and methodologies are worthwhile only if they are implemented. Too frequently one reads of a supposedly innovative program only to find on actual inspection a less exciting, more traditionally operated program than was depicted on paper. While poor program planning or the lack of adequate materials, equipment, or facilities often contribute to this problem, it is frequently the people who were called on to make the program work who have failed. In many cases, instructional and support personnel are not adequately prepared to fulfill their responsibilities.

Innovative teacher education programs of the kind discussed in this book demand a redefinition of roles within the learning process. If an individual has functioned successfully for a number of years in the lockstep approach of most current programs and is himself a product of such a program, he cannot be expected blithely to accept the innovations discussed here. Even if personnel accepted these innovations completely, one could not expect them to adopt new patterns of behavior without assistance.

So far we have mentioned only the situations in which a currently employed person can fill a particular new role. Smoothly functioning strategies of the kinds described above will require a whole class of personnel not often found in educational institutions. These are the support personnel, the people who do no actual instructing but, for example, design and construct educational materials, program and run computers, review data concerning individual and program progress, and carry out necessary redesign functions within the program system.

In order to ensure successful transfer to a new program, we must devise specific role descriptions for all jobs within the program system. These job descriptions must then be communicated to the various personnel in an appropriate, explicit, and public way. Staff development activities must be instituted so that current and new personnel will understand not only the requirements and responsibilities of their new roles, but also the reasons those roles are appropriate. Furthermore, they must understand the nature of the system so that they can understand where and how they fit into it. This phase of program development can be particularly stressful for current personnel, for eventually each individual must decide for himself whether he can fit into the new program. He must realize that, in a very real sense, he must play new roles or find other employment for which he is better suited.

There are at least three fundamental changes implied in the methodologies discussed above.

1. The most basic change is the recognition of student learning as self-initiated and self-guided. Instructional personnel will have to deal with this on a daily basis both in and out of class. The ideal implies a basic trust in the student that has too often been lacking in the college environment.

2. Instructional personnel will have to accept other program personnel—many of whom will not be credentialed college faculty— as peers with particular skills that are valuable to the program.

3. There must be a shift in the faculty reward structure. Teaching as an activity must be given status along with research and publishing. Extensive work with school inservice programs should also be considered in promotional policies. Colleges must have promotional policies that recognize these assumptions and reward personnel for what they do to serve program and student needs. Further, the reward system must recognize the contributions of faculty members in situations increasingly characterized by team arrangements.

In hiring personnel for a new program, it must be made clear that they are being hired to perform a certain set of functions within an operating system. For example, if a certain instructional module calls for specific kinds of instructor-student interaction, the instructor cannot "do his own thing," because his students would be penalized. In practice this means that hiring will be a process of matching an individual's unique capabilities with a particular set of responsibilities in which the individual feels comfortable. This simply extends the concept of differentiated staffing to higher education. People are hired to do what they do best and like to do, not what they have to do regardless of competency or interest.

In summary, innovative programs will cause a reorientation of instructional and support personnel. This reorientation will be best accomplished through the use of specific job descriptions and long-term staff development. The program designer should keep in mind that the result of such processes must be a job structure in which personnel do what they are most comfortable doing and do best and are appropriately rewarded. The program designer should not assume that everyone can adapt to such a structure.

References

Arends, Robert L., John A. Masla & Wilford A. Weber. *Handbook for the Development of Instructional Modules in Competency-Based Teacher Education Programs.* Buffalo, N.Y.: Center for the Study of Teaching, 1971.

6

Designing the Management Subsystem

Richard T. Coffing

Dale G. Hamreus

Chapter Objectives

The reader will be able to: (1) define the purpose and major elements of the management subsystem in a competency based teacher education program, (2) identify major functions in an organizational system and the general relationships between the management function and other functions, (3) identify principal steps to follow in producing a management design, and (4) identify substeps for solving a particular problem.

Introduction

A new set of methods for designing teacher education programs is explained in this volume. When competency based programs are developed using these methods, one can expect them to be more complicated than most current programs. Some of the differences may be quite pronounced; for instance, the new programs will be characterized by more variety, more data, more decisions, more problems, and more personal and organizational interrelationships. There will be greater differentiation of roles, and the students, employers, and faculty will face unprecedented opportunities for choice and influence.

Because competency based programs will be more complex, they will have management requirements that will be unfamiliar to many teacher educators. This chapter has been written to help the reader anticipate some of the new requirements and provide for them.

Definition of the Management Function

In order for any kind of program to accomplish its objectives, it has to be managed. People have to solve the problems that get in the way; the purpose of management is to ensure that this problem solving is accomplished.

When a teacher education program is viewed as a system, management can be considered one of its subsystems. Like the other subsystems, it needs to be designed; it will have inputs, outputs, processes, and feedback of information for decision making.

Unlike other subsystems, management's primary concern is the well-being of the whole system because it is responsible for integrating all the major parts into a goal-achieving combination. The distinguishing inputs to management can be called *organizational problems:* those observed discrepancies between a program objective or intended output and the actual performance or actual output of a subsystem or component. The distinguishing outputs of management are *organizational solutions,* or actions designed to reduce a discrepancy between intended and actual performance. Organizational solutions often find expression as *decision rules,* such as policies, which are applicable not just to a single problem but to a class of problems. Management's processes are the coordination and control operations through which an organizational problem is raised; potential solutions are generated and assessed; and a solution is selected, implemented, evaluated, and revised.

When program objectives have been specified clearly and completely, feedback information can be obtained at two levels of management performance. Information about the first level addresses the question, How effective is any particular solution in solving a particular problem? This helps to improve individual solutions. Information about the other level addresses the question, How well is the management subsystem fulfilling its purpose in the system? These data are helpful for redesigning management for the benefit of the whole. Feedback information can also be called *evaluation information* and *data for decision making.*

In concluding this definition, we want to emphasize one of its implications. When management is designed according to our definition in conjunction with the other components of the teacher education program, something quite unusual and valuable can happen: the management function itself can be closely examined with the scrutiny that managers usually direct toward others. The point is, management itself should be managed.

The Functions that Management Manages: Conceptual Models

As defined in this volume, the primary purpose of a teacher education program is to produce teachers possessing certain specified competencies. Therefore, the management subsystem must concern itself with all the organizational functions necessary to accomplish that purpose. Program designers should proceed from some overall conceptual framework of organizational functions; as examples, we shall present two different conceptual models. Both of them illustrate general conceptual completeness, which is a necessary foundation for a competency based program. The differences between them reflect the variety of concepts and terminology in the emerging study of the management of teacher education: a real condition facing the teacher educator today.

The first model has been adapted from Stanley Young's conceptualization for a teacher education program, based on his study of public service and business organizations.[1] The model is concerned with the following organizational functions: (1) demand analysis, (2) design, (3) financial analysis, (4) consensual analysis, (5) authorization, (6) resource acquisition, (7) promotion, (8) program delivery, (9) evaluation, and (10) management (system design). Together, these functions comprise a continuous, cyclical "organizational programing system,"[2] as shown in figure 1.

Demand Analysis

Organizational programing logically begins with demand analysis, the purpose of which is to determine specifically "who wants what." To fulfill the demand analysis function, program designers must examine the expectations of many clients, including teacher candidates, inservice teachers, recruiters, regulatory agencies, and the

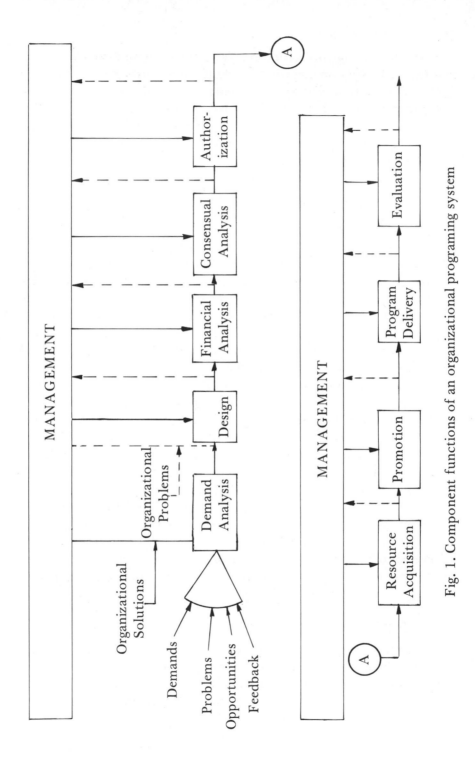

Fig. 1. Component functions of an organizational programing system

various publics served by schools. Even the faculty can be considered clients: internal clients. In addition, the program has to identify alternative futures for which students may need preparation. Finally, the program must use feedback information about its actual output. All these are demands on the program. When clients want services—for example, a community wants teachers with certain competencies—the demands can be viewed as opportunities for program development. Of course, problems occur, too: clients change, their expectations change, and program components fail to accomplish all the decision makers intended. Thus, the demand analysis function represents the continual formulation of problems and opportunities.

Design

Analyzed demand data serve as inputs to the design function, which is to produce new programs and revisions responsive to the demands facing the organization. Here is where the curriculum-instruction, support, and evaluation subsystems are designed; the design of management can be separately considered, as we shall see. Essentially, most of this book deals with the design function.

Financial Analysis

The purpose of this function is to estimate the probable costs and benefits of alternative program designs and to provide decision makers with a financial data base for their decisions. Depending on the problem, this activity may be simple or complex, perhaps involving computer simulation modeling of program proposals.

Consensual Analysis

Having financial data is not enough for effective program decision making. A program decision would be deficient if it could not or would not foreseeably be implemented as intended by the decision makers. Therefore, the purpose of the consensual analysis function is to provide decision makers primarily with nonfinancial data about the possible consequences of proposed designs as perceived by the people who are likely to be affected. What are their opinions about the value of proposed program changes, the feasibility of implementation, the willingness of the participants to cooperate? How do they think a proposal can be modified to improve its value? These are questions that need to be answered before a design or a redesign is authorized.

Authorization

This function represents the selection of the particular designs to be implemented. If the other organizational functions are fully developed, the authorization function will require little time and energy because most of the work leading to effective decision making will already be done.

Resource Acquisition

This function includes hiring and training staff, purchasing supplies and equipment, and performing other appropriate personnel and purchasing activities. Obviously, parts of the function may be performed by different organizational components.

Promotion

This function includes informing clients about the programs available for their benefit and giving internal participants whatever guidance and direction they need to make the program work.

Program Delivery

The purpose of this function is to deliver the curriculum-instruction; most people think of this as the main business of the teacher education organization. Of course, effective program delivery cannot happen without development of the other functions.

Evaluation

The purpose of this function is to provide feedback information to decision makers for use in revising and improving the program. When there are discrepancies between what is happening and what was supposed to happen, these discrepancies or problems must be fed back to the other functions for resolution. When evaluation data is used systematically to modify the activities leading to goal achievement, or even to modify the goals so that they are more achievable, the whole teacher education organization becomes a kind of learning system: a system that is capable of learning from its own behavior. See chapter 8 for further details on program evaluation.

Management (System Design)

The management or system design function designs and redesigns the other functions, which is another way of saying that management produces organizational solutions to organizational problems. The management function coordinates and integrates all the organizational functions so that the program accomplishes its intended purposes, e.g., to produce teachers possessing certain specified competencies. Following our presentation of the next model, we shall describe a method for performing part of this function, using the example of designing a coordination and control system.

The second organizational model for teacher education, adapted from the ComField Model[3] and shown in figure 2, is divided into subsystems and components as follows:

1. Curriculum-Instruction
   a. Instructional Objectives
   b. Instructional Design and Development
   c. Instructional Operations
2. Support
   a. Information Management
   b. Staff
   c. Cost Accounting
   d. Supply
   e. Data Generation
3. Changeover
   a. Program Accommodation
   b. Program Dissemination
4. Management
   a. Program Policy
   b. Program Execution
   c. Program Adaptation

Curriculum-Instruction

The three central boxes in figure 2 refer to curriculum-instruction components.

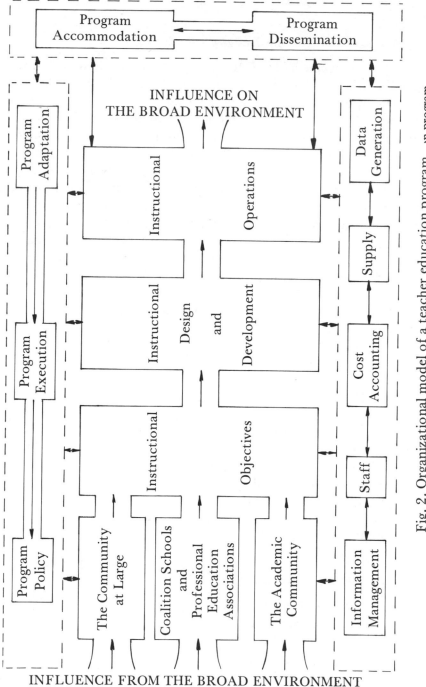

Fig. 2. Organizational model of a teacher education program   on program

Instructional Objectives

This function concerns specification of the objectives or outcomes expected from the program, based on the representative inputs of virtually everyone to be influenced by the educational program.

Instructional Design and Development

This function involves (1) specifying the curriculum-instruction intended to achieve the defined objectives, while considering the range of differences among learners; and (2) translating the specifications into learning packages. When appropriate, the function includes field testing and revision of the learning packages until achievement of the objectives is reasonably assured.

Instructional Operations

The operations function directs the teaching-learning interactions, including students' movement through the program consistent with a personalized, field centered, and competency based program.

Support

The lower row of boxes in figure 2 shows the support functions serving all other functions in the organization.

Information Management

The information function helps persons and groups in the organization to identify their information needs and designs and operates information systems for meeting those needs.

Staff

The staff function includes the selection and training of personnel; determination of rank, promotion, salary, and tenure policies; and promotion of staff welfare.

Cost Accounting

This function provides the accounting data, cost estimates, and financial analyses required for program decision making.

Supply

The supply function includes acquisition of supplies and maintenance of the nonhuman resources of the program, e.g., space, equipment and materials.

Data Generation

The data generation function identifies the organization's needs for research and evaluation data and designs, conducts, and reports research and evaluation studies. Since different decision makers—for example, students and program developers—require different data, this function must be just as concerned with who is to use the data as with what data are needed.

Changeover

The two boxes on the right side of figure 2 represent changeover functions that are useful when many institutions and agencies are jointly involved in changing from one educational program to another.

Program Accommodation

The accommodation function assures that no schism occurs between those developing the new programs and those maintaining an existing program during the transition period.

Program Dissemination

The dissemination function provides information about the program on request or by initiation.

Management

Finally, the top row of boxes in figure 2 show this model's management functions, providing for integration and coordination of the overall program.

Program Policy

In order to guide the subsystems of the organization, the policy function establishes written policy statements acceptable to the several constituencies comprising the program.

Program Execution

Considered the most crucial of all the functions in this model, the executive function coordinates and guides the translation of policies into operational activities. The executive function is related to the other functions as a conductor is related to a symphony orchestra.

Program Adaptation

This function monitors all program aspects, designing or redesigning the weak or failing parts. It must interact effectively with the data generation, information, and executive functions to fulfill its purposes. Figure 3 illustrates the adaptive-corrective capability essential to the whole program under this model.

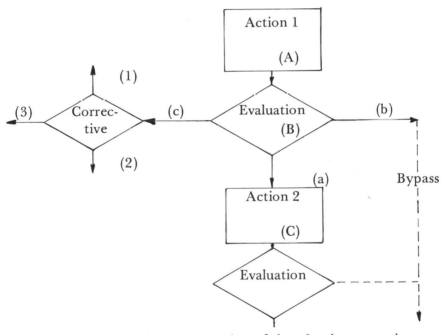

Fig. 3. Schematic representation of the adaptive-corrective nature of the management system

Figure 3 shows that after a specific action (A) occurs in the program, an evaluation (B) is made, resulting in three options. Option (a) provides normal forward progress to the next planned action and implies that the planned program is appropriate. Option (b) provides bypass directly to some later planned action and implies that a portion of the plan is redundant and can be omitted in this instance. Option (c) indicates need for corrective action to be taken and implies that the current plan is deficient. Three corrective alternatives are possible: (1) modifications of preceding actions, (2) modification of succeeding action(s), or (3) abandonment of that action chain because it fails to serve the program.

A Design Method and Resulting
Coordination and Control System

Accepting a general concept of organizational functions and recognizing a need for an adaptive-corrective capability, the teacher educator may ask whether program effectiveness can be ensured simply by adopting some specific model of "good organizational structure." Unfortunately, the problem is too complex for so simple a solution; other important variables must be considered, such as the tasks to be done, the technology to be employed, and the people who participate.[4] Integrating these variables is not a simple job for management, because structure, tasks, technology, and people are highly interdependent, and "change in any one," as Harold Leavitt notes, "will most probably result in compensatory (or retaliatory) change in others."[5]

Most of the management problems of a teacher education program will not be solved by having someone outside the program prescribe the jobs to be done, the organizational structure, the methods, and the participants. On the other hand, neither will they be solved by having the program director alone integrate the many variables and functions. What is needed is a set of minimal, regularized procedures for problem solving that continuously spread the necessary work throughout the organization. In the next few pages, we shall describe a method for designing such a "coordination and control system."

Actually, we shall describe an iterative, nine-step method for designing the management subsystem and, at the same time, demonstrate that process by hypothetically designing a coordination and control system. The description reflects a logical sequence of steps, but in actual operation the process is dynamic and cyclical. We recommend that teacher educators seriously consider using not only this design method but also the hypothetical coordination and control system presented here. Therefore we have designed the hypothetical system to mirror the design method so that the reader will have some practice with both before having to make a decision about their value in a particular program.

Perhaps the key assumption behind our presentation is that the designer should begin simply. It usually will be easier to add detail to the design after evaluating what it can and cannot do than it will be to start with a complex design and then try to find out how to make it work. For competency based programs, we believe this assumption will be helpful most of the time.

Suppose that you are the prospective designer of a new, competency based teacher education program and, further, that you accept the organizational programing model shown in figure 1. In fact, you like the terminology, believe the model is complete enough at that general level, and are willing to hear about the necessary implementing activities. We know that if we were to recommend specific activities for implementing the model, you would quickly and correctly see that they do not fit your organizational situation. Therefore, we choose instead to describe a method you can use to design the activities yourself. It may be helpful to think of this method as a tool for breaking down the general conceptual model into specific operations.

Step 1. Identify Some Things the Management Subsystem Must Accomplish in the Program and Define Some Performance Measures

You do not have to know all your management needs at the outset; to begin with, write down in one-line statements the needs you think of. For example, suppose you identify as a critical need, "to coordinate and control the problem-solving activities in my organization." Then, for each need you list, think of some indicator that you would accept as evidence of achievement; for instance, "my feelings of better problem solutions and an absence of complaints from the staff." Fine. Fuzzy, subjective criteria are not unreasonable at this stage. As you operate the management subsystem, if this need is really important to you, you will refine the criteria and probably add to them. The point is, do not look for perfection early in the game; *just begin.*

Step 2. Search for a Solution

If there is no solution already on file or otherwise known to

you, e.g., an appropriate policy or procedure, you may have to design one. Assuming you must invent a system for coordination and
control, you might begin by breaking down the organizational functions of the model into analogous problem-solving activities. An
example of such a breakdown is shown below.

Organizational Functions	*Problem-Solving Activities*
Demand Analysis	Identify organizational problems and opportunities.
	Diagnose organizational problems and opportunities.
Design	Search for solutions.
Financial Analysis	Estimate costs and benefits of proposed solutions.
Consensual Analysis	Analyze proposals from perspective of people affected.
Authorization	Decide whether to implement a proposed solution.
Resource Acquisition	Acquire resources to implement the authorized solution.
Promotion	Guide and direct those who implement the solution.
Program Delivery	Operate the solution.
Evaluation	Evaluate the solution.

Since problem-solving activities must fit together in a system,
let us suppose you think of some logical components such as

1. A way to raise problems and opportunities

2. A way to schedule the problem-solving activities

3. A way to store information on problems, opportunities, and
solutions

4. Some kind of flow diagram to assist you and others in understanding the process

5. Somebody to do the work

Because you are emphasizing progress rather than perfection,
you next work out some simple forms and procedures and then cast
your imagination forward to see how they might be put to use. You
might envision the problem/opportunity form set out below as a way
of initiating actions under the proposed system. Any person associated with the program may fill out the form and give it to the
coordinator of the system. Sometimes the coordinator fills it out
himself if the problem or opportunity comes from an outside source.
The coordinator enters the item in the log devised for scheduling
purposes (see figure 4), and he may create a file for information
storage if the item appears to be an important one that has not been
considered before. He then routes the item through the problem-

Problem/Opportunity Form

Statement of the Problem or Opportunity:

Causes:

Suggested Solutions:

From: Telephone:
* *
Date Received: Sender Acknowledged:
Referred for Solution to:
Disposition of Problem/Opportunity:

solving process. Together, these components make up a rudimentary coordination and control system.

Figure 5 shows how the flow of work might look for one item coming into your imaginary future program. Suppose this particular opportunity comes from an "external client," a large school system that has not previously had a very close relationship to your institution, the state university. (Of course, the opportunity might also come from an "internal client," such as a faculty member or student; futurist studies; or evaluation of the current program.) They want to start a districtwide inservice training program in competency based curricula at the secondary level, and they want your institution to design and install the program by next fall, under contract.

The coordinator receives from the director of teacher education

Problem/Opportunity Log

P/O No.	Identification: To	Date	Sched. Compl.	Actual Compl.	Search for Solution: To	Date	Sched. Compl.	Actual Compl.	Financial Analysis: To	Date	Sched. Compl.	Actual Compl.

P/O No.	Consensual Analysis: To	Date	Sched. Compl.	Actual Compl.	Decision: To	Date	Sched. Compl.	Actual Compl.	Resource Acquisition: To	Date	Sched. Compl.	Actual Compl.

P/O No.	Direction and Guidance: To	Date	Sched. Compl.	Actual Compl.	Operation: To	Date	Sched. Compl.	Actual Compl.	Evaluation: To	Date	Sched. Compl.	Actual Compl.

Fig. 4. Scheduling log

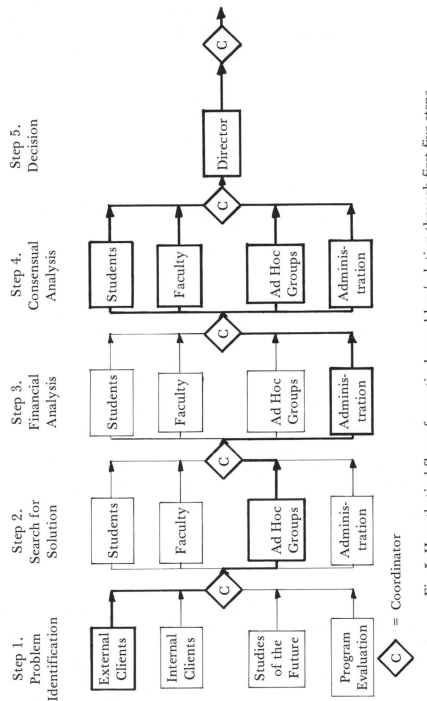

Fig. 5. Hypothetical flow of a particular problem/solution through first five steps

a copy of the district's request. He checks the files for similar previous opportunities; if he does not find any, he fills out a problem/opportunity form. In consultation with the director, the coordinator refers the item to an ad hoc committee composed of three faculty members with previous inservice consulting experience and two graduate students who have been studying the problems of preservice-inservice continuity in teacher education. The committee diagnoses the opportunity through meetings with school district staff. Then, working with an assistant superintendent, a principal, and a department chairman from the school district, the committee develops a plan and an estimated budget. By established procedure, the dean's finance specialist reviews the budget, adjusts several expense items, adds an overhead figure, and gives the proposal to the coordinator. Because there have been some misunderstandings and disappointments in connection with previous contractual approvals, the coordinator knows that the proposal must be checked out "across campus" as well as by the College of Education people who will be primarily involved. (The director, of course, does not want to make a decision that is likely to be vetoed, either officially by some other authority or unofficially by several key staff members simply withholding their services.) The consensus step is deliberately thorough; among other things, it turns up the fact that one faculty member, who was not contacted in the planning even though his time was tentatively committed, will be on leave next year. The proposal is revised to substitute more graduate assistants and is given to the director for his decision, which is to go ahead.

This is enough on the inservice training example to give you the idea of searching for a solution. Now we shall continue with step 3 of the general model.

Step 3. Analyze the Expected Financial Costs and
Benefits of the Proposed Solution

You will want to estimate at least the direct costs, such as the coordinator's time and materials and the time of persons participating in diagnosis, design, consensual analysis, and evaluation of solutions, and perhaps make some guess at indirect costs, such as 10 percent for heat, light, building maintenance, and business office services. In the beginning, it may not be clear how your cost figures and benefit calculations, if any, can be used. This is because educational organizations have rarely identified the economic value of their programs or used such data for decision making. Development of that capability might be one of the purposes of the proposed coordination system.

Step 4. Get Consensus Information from Persons
Likely to Be Affected by the Proposed Solution

You will have to canvass the people likely to be affected by the proposal, asking such questions as: Would they use it? How do they view its potential effects on themselves and on the program? Do they confirm the financial analysis? What modifications do they suggest? It may then be necessary to recycle step 2 and do some redesign work.

Some of the negative reactions you may get to the proposed coordination and control system are: "The terminology is jargon"; "it's too rationalistic—people just don't work that way"; "our present methods are probably better or at least good enough"; "the 'consensus' business is just a game, because the director usually has his mind made up beforehand, anyway"; and "if every little problem has to go through the same procedures, we won't have time left to get any work done." But you will usually find that even the people who reacted negatively are willing to give it a try, if it is kept simple and operated for a trial period culminating, perhaps, in a faculty vote.

On the other hand, some of the favorable reactions to the proposal might be: "The process seems knowable and accessible rather than mysterious or devious"; "problems will be looked into in an orderly way, instead of the present random activity"; "it can avoid some of our tedious large meetings and take advantage of ad hoc problem-solving groups"; "it seems flexible and adaptable to the particular problems at hand"; and "individuals can be heard."

Step 5. Make a Decision

If you like the solution, it is acceptable to others, it appears implementable, and its benefits seem likely to exceed its costs in your terms, then implement it. Otherwise, drop it or go back to step 2 for redesign. Notice that making the decision does not take long, because the spadework and pre-evaluation have already been done. Decision making can be almost the least time-consuming step in this design method, because the decision maker does not have to perform all the other functions as well. Moreover, the steps following the decision are made easier by the previous work.

Step 6. Acquire the Personnel, Materials, and
Facilities Required for the Solution

In the hypothetical case of the coordination and control
system, there may still be work to do to complete the design and
produce the forms, logs, and detailed instructions. Also, the coordinator has to be designated: possibly an assistant to the director of
teacher education.

Step 7. Give Direction and Guidance to
All Persons Who Will or Should Use the Solution

The people whose problems and opportunities the authorized
system is intended to handle must be informed that the system exists
and taught how to use it. Persons who will be involved as solution
designers need to know what is expected of them; this is true for all
roles in the system.

Step 8. Operate the Solution

Put the coordination and control system into effect, starting
without fanfare and with the simplest problem that anyone raises in
earnest. That way you give yourself a chance to work out the inevi-
table "bugs" under the most favorable conditions.

Step 9. Evaluate the Solution in
Terms of Expectations

Is the solution accomplishing the things it is supposed to accomplish? In our hypothetical example, is the system succeeding as
measured by your "feelings and the absence of complaints from the
staff"? If you find discrepancies between your expectations and the
system's actual performance, you will probably either modify the
system in some way or change your expectations.

Return to Step 1. Identify Management
Needs and Define Performance Measures

This is the same function that was discussed above, but now
you have some evaluation data about the solution you tried on your
first problem. You may choose to refine the solution to that problem, or you may want to venture into a second management need.
Either way, you can cycle through the steps of the design process
again and again to accomplish your purposes.

In concluding this discussion, we hope that not only the logic but also the particulars of this approach will prove helpful to you.[6] This approach will not be effective for everyone, and the determination of its appropriateness for you is, of course, yours to make. The art and science of management design does not have to be obscure and inaccessible to the teacher educator. We believe that the field should be entered through simple methods such as this and that, when it is, the work can be both productive and fun.

Guidelines for Designing Management
Activities to Solve a Particular Problem

When a problem has been identified, as in step 1 of the preceding method, a solution typically needs to be designed (step 2). Suppose, for example, that we need to identify what the program's goals should be from the perspective of its clients. We suggest the following four guidelines for use in designing a solution:

1. Identify the attributes of a successful solution. In other words, what should the solution look like? In terms of our example, these attributes might include:

a. The solution would involve obtaining statements of desirable program goals from representatives of all clienteles of the program.

b. Goals would have to be ranked in some priority order from the clients' perspectives.

c. The goals and priorities would have to be synthesized into a composite picture.

d. The process must be repeated periodically to maintain sensitivity to what the clients believe are relevant goals.

2. Identify the resources necessary to achieve such a solution. Each aspect of the solution can be considered in terms of human and nonhuman resources. As an example of human resource considerations, in terms of obtaining clients' statements of goals for the program (attribute a. above), it may be critical to have representative views from (a) members of the community served by the schools cooperating with the teacher education program; (b) teachers, administrators, and school board members from the cooperating schools; (c) faculty of the teacher education institution, (d) students preparing to be teachers, and (e) members of the state's educational professional associations.

3. Identify the constraints on the solution. If too little money is available for a total solution, whatever that might be, a partial solution may have to suffice. Other constraints might include the time available to complete the tasks, the willingness of people to cooperate, the political climate in the area, and so on.

4. Specify the activities necessary to achieve the solution. In our example this might include spelling out the details of identifying clients; selecting representatives and convening them if desired; designing methods for obtaining their statements of goals for the program; and providing stipends, transportation, and meals for community representatives. Moreover, this step includes specifying what the various organizational functions must do. For example, the designer might ask the information function to get lists of names and backgrounds of prospective representatives and the staffing function to plan the training of representatives in specific techniques for specifying objectives.

By following these rough guidelines, the designer should be able to produce potentially workable solutions that are ready for the financial and consensual reviews suggested in steps 3 and 4 of the preceding section.

Summary

The success of competency based teacher education programs will be partially contingent on effective management processes. To handle the differences between present programs and proposed new designs, creative management designs will be required. The management subsystem must be grounded in a conceptual framework that includes all functions of the organization.

In the final analysis, the program staff will have to do most of the design work. But with the methods and guidelines of this chapter, we believe they can reasonably ensure the manageability of their program.

Footnotes

1. As conceptualized during preparation of the management design reported in James M. Cooper et al., *A Feasibility Study on the Model Elementary Teacher Education Program*, U.S. Office of Education Contract No. OEC-0-9-310417-4040(010) (Amherst: University of Massachusetts, 1969); the con-

cepts are more extensively discussed in Stanley Young & Richard T. Coffing, "Organizational Programming and the University," Working paper for the President's Committee on the Future University of Massachusetts (Amherst: University of Massachusetts, 1971).

2. Young and Coffing, "Organizational Programming."

3. Adapted from H. Del Shalock & James R. Hale, eds., *A Competency Based, Field-Centered, Systems Approach to Elementary Teacher Education,* U.S. Office of Education Contract No. OEC-0-8-089022-3318(010) (Portland, Oreg.: Northwest Regional Educational Laboratory et al., 1968).

4. Harold J. Leavitt, "Applied Organizational Change in Industry: Structural, Technical and Human Approaches," in *New Perspectives in Organizational Research,* ed. W. W. Cooper, H. J. Leavitt & M. W. Shelly II (New York: John Wiley & Sons, 1964), pp. 55–71.

5. Ibid., p. 56.

6. To further explore the basic approach, see Stanley Young, *Management: A Systems Analysis* (Glenview, Ill.: Scott, Foresman, 1966); Kathryn V. Feyereisen, A. John Fiorino & Arlene T. Nowak, *Supervision and Curriculum Renewal: A Systems Approach* (New York: Appleton-Century-Crofts, 1970).

References

Churchman, C. West. *The Systems Approach.* New York: Dell, 1968.

Cleland, David I. & William R. King. *Systems, Organizations, Analysis, Management: A Book of Readings.* New York: McGraw-Hill, 1969.

Cook, Desmond L. *Educational Project Management.* Columbus, Ohio: Charles E. Merrill, 1971.

Corrigan, Robert E. & Roger A. Kaufman. *Why System Engineering.* Belmont, Calif.: Fearon, 1965.

Feyereisen, Kathryn V., A. John Fiorino & Arlene T. Nowak. *Supervision and Curriculum Renewal: A Systems Approach.* New York: Appleton-Century-Crofts, 1970.

Hersey, Paul & Kenneth H. Blanchard. *Management of Organizational Behavior: Utilizing Human Resources.* Englewood Cliffs, N.J.: Prentice-Hall, 1969.

McGregor, Douglas, *The Professional Manager.* Edited by Caroline McGregor and Warren G. Bennis. New York: McGraw-Hill, 1967.

Schein, Edgar H. *Organizational Psychology.* Englewood Cliffs, N.J.: Prentice-Hall, 1965.

Young, Stanley. *Management: A Systems Analysis.* Glenview, Ill.: Scott, Foresman, 1966.

7

Designing Support Subsystems

H. Del Schalock

James M. Cooper

Chapter Objectives

The reader will be able to: (1) explain the structure and functions of support subsystems, (2) describe processes by which support subsystems might be designed and developed, and (3) understand the support system presented for illustrative purposes.

Introduction

In broad terms, every teacher education system involves three interacting subsystems: the instructional subsystem, the management subsystem, and the support subsystems. The relationship between these aspects of a total program is illustrated schematically in figure 1.

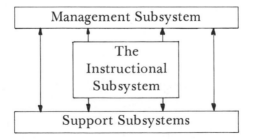

Fig. 1. Subsystems basic to all teacher education systems

While the curriculum-instruction subsystem is the essence of a teacher education program, it must be managed and it must be supported in a number of ways.

In traditional teacher education programs, support functions are manned by persons such as administrators, registrars, counselors, and maintenance personnel. In a competency based, personalized, field centered, and data dependent teacher education program, these same supporting functions must also be performed, but they assume a somewhat different and vastly expanded form.

The purpose of this chapter is to provide an overview of the support subsystems needed by a teacher education program of the kind envisioned in this book, to offer guidelines for the development of support components that can carry out the program's operations, and to provide, for illustrative purposes, more detailed specifications of a staff selection and development support subsystem that has been designed for application in a competency based program.

A note of caution: the support subsystems as they are described here should be viewed as somewhat idealized. They are based on the assumption of a program that is fully committed to the kind of program outlined in this book. They are also based on the assumption of a resource base that will permit the full development and operation of such a program. Neither assumption, of course, need be true. Any given teacher education program at a given time will be uneven in its commitments to the various aspects of the program being proposed. It will also be uneven in the extent to which it can implement its commitments. For example, the staff of a program may be committed to a field based and personalized mode of instruction and may have the resources needed to implement it, but they may have solved the logistical problems only for the personalized aspect of the program within the college context and been unable to solve the logistics of field centered instruction. As a consequence, some readers may find our proposals unrealistic or unattainable; to others, however, the same proposals may appear quite reasonable.

Our intent in this chapter is to outline the ideal; recognizing that the ideal may never be realized, we shall also offer suggestions about how a program might function with less than the ideal. Our premise is that the elaboration of support components can be compromised, but their existence cannot.

Support Subsystems

A wide variety of support operations must be maintained if the kind of teacher education program envisioned is to function. These include management of information; generation of data on program effectiveness; generation of data on program cost; maintenance of equipment, supplies, and facilities; selection and admission of students; and selection and training of staff.

The formal structure created to carry out these functions, however, and the number and organization of components within a particular structure are arbitrary. Because of preferences or constraints, one program may provide for its support operations through three subsystems, while another may choose to do so through six or eight. The point of concern is that all the necessary support operations for each unique program are provided, not how they are provided.

For the purposes of this chapter, it is proposed that the support functions needed to operate a competency based, field centered, personalized, and data dependent teacher education program be provided through five support subsystems: (1) program evaluation and student assessment, (2) cost accounting, (3) maintenance, (4) student selection and welfare, and (5) staff selection, training, and welfare. The rationale for and functions of these subsystems are described briefly in the following paragraphs. Suggestions about their design and operation appear later in the chapter.

Program Evaluation and Student Assessment

The information demands of a competency based, field centered, personalized, and data dependent teacher education program are extremely high. As students progress through the instructional program, they must have information that permits them and their instructors to assess their progress and make appropriate choices among learning steps. Advisors must be able to examine performance histories in order to counsel with sensitivity. Instructional program development personnel must have information about the effectiveness of given instructional modules. Registrars must be kept abreast of student progress; cost-benefit data must be available to those responsible for the adaptation and execution of the program; and supply orders must be updated. The program evaluation and student assessment subsystem must be able to meet these and dozens of other information needs, for sound decision making depends on sound data.

In brief, the evaluation subsystem must be able to provide every person involved in the program with the information needed to make critical decisions in relation to the program. This is the case for students as well as instructional staff and for support personnel as well as management personnel. Chapter 8 provides more details regarding the need for and use of information in program evaluation and student performance assessment.

Cost Accounting Subsystem

The general movement toward accountability in education leads to the conclusion that education in general must demonstrate a more rigorous stance regarding returns for dollars invested. This requires more than showing that the dollars available to a program were spent "judiciously" or "honestly." It requires that actual resource expenditures be attached to operations designed to bring about given outcomes or serve specified functions; it also requires evidence about the effectiveness of operations using those resources. In short, it requires program operation subject to "management by objectives," with cost-benefit measures being the primary criteria for judging the effectiveness of program operation.

A cost accounting subsystem is needed to allocate resources by program or function and monitor the actual resource consumption of a given program or function. Such a subsystem would assume the traditional functions of fiscal management and budgeting and would take on the characteristics of an accounting department in a corporate structure.

Maintenance Subsystem

In a personalized teacher education program, the materials, equipment, and space needs are considerably different from those in traditionally structured programs. Multiple learning stations must be provided for individuals, small groups, and occasional large groups of students. Materials are needed to support learning experiences that are a part of instructional modules. Assessment devices must be on hand or available on request. Moreover, equipment must be available to support all of the above. In addition, buildings and grounds must be maintained, supplies must be available for curriculum-instruction subsystem development, office supplies must be provided, and so forth. The maintenance subsystem attends to all these needs.

Student Selection and Welfare Subsystem

While a competency based, field centered, and personalized program need not select its students as carefully as traditional programs, there is a great concern for the ultimate selection of those to be graduated and certified and for the welfare of students within the program. In a competency based program, students are given every benefit of the doubt as to their ultimate ability to perform successfully within the program, and they may take as long as they need, within reasonable limits, to develop the required competencies. However, extremely careful assessment is made before allowing the student to assume responsibilities for the learning of children in the field or leave the program with initial or continuing certification.

Commitment to a personalized program requires a corresponding commitment to the welfare of individual students within it. Central to student welfare are sets of learning experiences that help students understand themselves as individuals within the context of a college setting, a field setting, and a professional education setting. A basic assumption for such a program is that the soundness of decision making within the program is directly related to the clarity of understanding students have about their goals, commitments, and preferences.

Staff Selection, Training, and Welfare Subsystem

In a teacher education program that takes on the characteristics of the program being proposed, staff roles and functions differ considerably from those in a traditionally designed program. Staff are no longer primarily lecturers; rather, they become a combination of instructor in the traditional sense, instructional systems developer, advisor, negotiator, data generator, and researcher. Staff who are accustomed to functioning in a traditional context will need to be extensively retrained to function in the emerging context. Moreover, the program may need to add staff with new capabilities, such as formally trained evaluation personnel, information management personnel, and cost accountants. In all cases, the selection of new staff must be done with careful reference to the demands of the program.

Designing Support Systems

The first reaction to both the concept and the number of support subsystems that have been proposed can be one of dismay. The very term *subsystem* has impersonal, mechanistic, and dehumanizing overtones, and the sheer number of subsystems described suggests the possibility of a distorted emphasis on operational requirements. From the point of view of those who have attempted to design or implement such a program, however, this is not the case. In fact, just the reverse is true; the various supporting functions that have been described ensure that instruction will be personalized, the program will be accountable, and viable field relationships will be established. In this sense, support subsystems are the vehicles of a personalized, data dependent, and field centered program and therefore must be planned and provided for with the same care as the curriculum-instruction subsystem.

In thinking about the design of support components, three points should be kept in mind:

1. Just as the clustering of functions within a given subsystem is arbitrary, so is its structure. Each subsystem must be designed to accommodate the idiosyncrasies of a particular program.

2. A number of factors must be considered in the design of any subsystem. These factors should include (a) the mission of the subsystem, (b) the necessary functions to carry out the subsystem's mission, (c) the structure of the subsystem, (d) the composition of the subsystem, and (e) the linkages between the curriculum-instruction and management subsystems and the other supporting subsystems within the overall program.

3. The formal design statement should explain the rationale for each component and specify a plan of implementation.

The Mission of the Subsystem

The design of any support subsystem must begin with a clear statement of its mission. In this context, *mission* is defined as the outcomes to be achieved by the subsystem. These outcomes are the specific outputs or products for which the subsystem is held responsible and serve as criteria against which its performance can be measured. Lack of a clear statement of mission will severely handicap the design. Since the mission of any supporting subsystem is determined by the demands of the total program, it is not possible to specify all the outcomes of a given subsystem until the total program has been defined. Nevertheless, the best possible mission statement must be made early in the design phase.

Functions of the Subsystem

For purposes of the present volume, *functions* is defined as the largest classes of activity that must be performed to carry out the mission of the subsystem. These classes of activity are simply descriptive labels for interrelated sets of actions. The specification of functions is always an arbitrary matter, and they will change from time to time and from program to program. It is useful to specify them, however, because they identify the kinds of work to be done and thereby permit the ordering of necessary personnel, resources, and time.

Structure of the Subsystem

Functions cannot occur without a structure. In order to organize people, resources, and time to carry out the functions, some organizational-operational structuring must be provided. For purposes of this chapter, *structure* is defined as the organizational unit by which resources are assigned, outcomes are held accountable, and operations are managed. Like all aspects of program development, the structure of a particular subsystem will be determined by the needs, desires, and constraints of a particular program and will change as a program changes over time. The structure anticipated for the subsystem is an important consideration in the subsystem's design, however, and it should be specified early.

Composition of the Subsystem

The people who will operate a subsystem are critical factors in its design. Two factors need to be considered in their selection: (1) the competencies they bring to the subsystem in relation to the tasks that are to be carried out, and (2) the institutions and agencies or departments and schools that they represent. In combination, these two factors constitute the composition of the subsystem. *Composition* is defined here as the distribution of personnel within the subsystem according to competence and representation.

In a competency based, field centered, and personalized teacher education program the matters of competence and representation within support subsystems are critical. People responsible for the operation of the subsystem must be able to perform the functions required of them if the subsystem is to carry out its mission. In like terms, those people who are a part of or are affected by the subsystem must have a chance to influence it. This is not to say that all institutions and agencies or schools and departments involved in the program must be represented in every subsystem. It is important to recognize, however, that competence and representation must always be considered and that the two must be mixed appropriately in order for a given subsystem to function effectively over time.

Linkages Between Support Subsystems

The ways in which the support subsystems link with other subsystems in the program—including other support subsystems—must be clearly specified. Without such specification, it is impossible to identify the outputs that each must provide for the others, establish clear criteria against which they can be measured, or estimate accurately the resources needed for achievement of their missions. As in the case of mission statements, linkage statements cannot be complete until the total program is designed, but they should be spelled out as clearly as possible as soon as possible and continuously updated as the program evolves.

An Illustrative Design of a Support Subsystem

To help the reader understand what the specifications of a support subsystem might look like, we have included an example that outlines a staff selection and development subsystem.[1] Specifications such as these should be developed for each subsystem.

Staff Selection and Development

Mission
To select staff to meet the manpower demands of program management, instructional management, general support, and changeover functions; to orient new staff to the program and functions for which they will be responsible; to establish and maintain an inservice training program for the professional development

of all staff; to determine personnel policies for the rank, promotion, salary, and tenure of all staff; to provide means by which professional goals of staff can be identified, described, facilitated, and evaluated.

Tasks

1. Identify personnel capabilities needed to carry out the development of each program function.[2]

2. Identify criteria for personnel selection.

3. Identify and interview prospective staff.

4. Determine the appropriate personnel to meet specified manpower needs of program mechanisms.

5. Establish and maintain a personnel orientation program that is interrelated with the recruitment program but offers more detailed information and exposures to the program.

6. Assess general and specific personnel capabilities needed to perform professional tasks in carrying out specific program operations.

7. Specify general and specific personnel capabilities for which professional training is needed.

8. Organize a task force to design an inservice training program to meet general and specific professional training needs of staff.

9. Coordinate the development of an inservice training program by identifying and securing (a) program instructional staff, (b) instructional materials, and (c) instructional logistics.

10. Provide evaluation, feedback, and follow-up on the inservice training program to both trainers and trainees.

11. Modify the inservice training program on the basis of feedback about its effectiveness and clarification of the training needs within the proposed program.

12. Establish means whereby present personnel policies and practices of the college and the schools can be reviewed and modified wherever possible to accommodate the program ideal.

13. Solicit recommended personnel policies and practices from staff congruent with the commitments of the total program.

14. Specify personnel policies and practices that will be established and carried out.

15. Identify the professional goals of all staff or help staff to identify professional goals.

16. Determine goals that directly facilitate the program (both long-term and short-term) and identify acceptable indicators of their achievement.

17. Facilitate the attainment of the professional goals of personnel executing program tasks.

Rationale

One significant task in implementing the proposed program is to ensure that each individual involved can meet the responsibilities and challenges he will face. This will require a close fit between the proposed program objectives and the professional goals and commitments of staff who develop and operate the program.

The proposed program will require some unique new roles and functions from both college and school personnel. As a consequence, the staff selection and development function must receive critical attention. Among other things, this requires new ways of relating to colleagues in developing and operating the program.

Argyris indicates that managers are motivated by three basic assumptions in their behavior toward staff: (1) that staff are oriented toward objectives; (2) that productivity increases with rationality and decreases with emotionality; and (3) that commitment and loyalty are fostered through directions, controls, rewards, and penalties. He has also shown that these managerial assumptions have usually minimized personal feedback, expression of ideas and feelings, openness, and risk taking and have maximized negativism, invertedness, defensiveness, and inflexibility. In short, Argyris has demonstrated that the application of the traditional personnel principles has generally resulted in low interpersonal competence within organizations.[3]

In the proposed program, there is a commitment to overcome the negative consequences typically associated with traditional management procedures. Two steps are being taken in this regard:

1. Management practices are designed to maximize personal feedback, expression of ideas and feelings, openness, and risk taking and minimize negativism, invertedness, defensiveness, and inflexibility.

2. Staff selection and development procedures emphasize the value of the growth and development of each staff member taking part in the program.

In light of the kinds of demands to be made of staff in the proposed program, the aim of staff selection and development is to bring about a high degree of individuality, trust, competency, and internal commitment in all staff. The realization of this aim will require careful balance between staff selection, job design, and management procedures. All will need to be focused on promoting productiveness, satisfaction, and challenge within the execution of the proposed program.

Structure

A two-level structure: one level determines and executes personnel policies and practices within the multi-institutional coalition; and the other level prepares personnel to function proficiently in performing program management, instructional management, and general support tasks.

Composition

A director of staff selection and development will be primarily responsible for managing the design, implementation, development, and operation of the functions described. Therefore, the director must have experience in, and a close working relationship with, the multi-institutional coalition personnel programs. An additional direct responsibility of the director will be the identification, facilitation, and evaluation of staff professional goals that support the capability to carry out the program effectively and efficiently.

Assisting the director will be:

1. A personnel specialist in the recruitment and selection of staff

2. A personnel specialist in the orientation and training of staff

3. A cadre of staff trainers who also have responsibilities for designing and developing the functions to carry out (a) instructional management tasks, (b) program management tasks, and/or (c) general support tasks

4. Consulting representatives from the coalition (college and schools) and the state department of education who have ongoing responsibilities for personnel programs in their respective areas.

Implementation

A staff selection and development task force must design the operations for implementation. Time parameters must be set for the task force so that the design can be expected by a particular date.

Short-term, inservice training programs must be developed and carried out in accordance with the overall time framework in order to prepare staff to implement all functions.

Facilitating the professional goals of all program staff will require review, analysis, and recommendation procedures early in the development of the program. These activities will need to continue, but primarily for program evaluative purposes rather than design, development, and implementation. Once implemented, personnel evaluations will be continuous and must be coordinated with all functions.

Summary

This chapter has described the need for support subsystems to facilitate the accomplishment of the curriculum-instruction subsystem's purposes. The chapter has also described certain support functions that virtually every teacher education program needs, giving detailed specifications of a staff selection and development subsystem. The next chapter will describe one of the most critical support subsystems, evaluation.

Footnotes

1. This example was developed by Roger Sell and was taken from ComField elementary model, Phase II Final Report, *A Plan for Managing the Development, Implementation and Operation of a Model Elementary Teacher Education Program*, vol. 1, Oregon College of Education (Washington, D.C.: U.S. Government Printing Office, 1970), pp. 177–180.

2. The outcome of this task should be descriptions of (a) what each person in each of the functions is expected to do; (b) the personal characteristics or qualities that are judged important to each job, e.g., degree, experience, commitments, personal goals, professional goals, etc.; (c) the suggested salary for each job; (d) the types of available personnel who should be considered for specific jobs; and (e) any special qualifications that the jobs call for or that may not be present in available personnel.

3. Chris Argyris, *Human Nature and Organizational Realities* (1967).

8

Program Evaluation and Student Assessment

Norman R. Dodl

Chapter Objectives

The reader will be able to describe (1) the three major functions of an evaluation subsystem, (2) the relationship of the evaluation subsystem with the management subsystem, (3) how student assessment can be personalized for each trainee, and (4) how student assessment processes differ at the performance and consequence levels, as opposed to the knowledge level.

Introduction

The previous chapter has discussed the functions of support subsystems in a competency based teacher education program. One of the most crucial support subsystems in the operation of a data based program is the evaluation subsystem. It has been singled out for elaboration because of its central importance in a systems approach.

Feedback regarding student progress and program operation depends on the information that performance assessment must provide. Program management must use personnel and material resources in efficient ways if program outcomes are to be achieved in the face of shrinking educational budgets. Curriculum design and modification must be based on sound information rather than on the whim of a few "enlightened" professionals. Even the assumptions, goals, and objectives underlying and giving direction to a competency based teacher education program must be treated as untested hypotheses to be constantly reexamined and revised in the light of new information if relevance is to be maintained.

Within any program designed as a total system, provision must be made for the collection of information needed for program evaluation. In a competency based program the need to assess performance adds a major dimension to the already broad demands for information needed by the system design. Thus, evaluation is defined in this chapter as the generation and analysis of information that supports decision making relative to the accomplishment of desired outcomes. While it is possible to provide for such evaluation within other subsystems, this chapter presents a case for an evaluation subsystem that supports all other subsystems.

A competency based teacher education program is significantly different from traditional programs in that it is designed as a total system. Decision areas, decision agents, types of information, and sources of information are determined in advance as integral parts of the system designed. Efficient operation and regular program revision depend on system decisions; these decisions require that specific information be available at the right time to the appropriate decision makers.

Two basic categories of information are essential to the decision process: outcome and process discrepancies. The major product is a teacher who can demonstrate desired competencies. Because curriculum-instruction objectives are stated in terms of these competencies, it is critical to the student and to the program that discrepancies between competencies attained and competencies expected are regularly ascertained and analyzed. An evaluation subsystem can provide this information on outcome discrepancies.

Because efficient operation is a system requirement, the attainment of competencies (or the discrepany between attained and expected competencies) must be related to the processes by which they are produced and to the relative costs of producing them. The system proceeds or does not proceed according to design; it is important to management and curriculum designers to be kept informed about the discrepancy between the program's design and its actual operations. It is equally important to management to have accurate information about the costs actually incurred as compared with the projected costs. It is such information on process discrepancies which, when analyzed with outcome discrepancies, provides decision makers with the data needed to operate and redesign systems.[1]

It should be stressed here that the job of an evaluation team is to gather and to analyze relevant data for use by decision makers. This process should not become confused with the decision making process itself. Policy and operational decisions are made within the total system by the appropriate sets of decision agents. In all likelihood, those on the evaluation team will not also be involved in the decision process.

Although every program is unique in some respect, many of the decision areas will be similar from program to program. Certain decisions are common to all programs and will require similar kinds of data. Every subsystem of a competency based teacher education program requires decision making by a variety of decision agents. Every decision requires relevant information from a variety of sources. For instance, provision for the recruitment, selection, and counseling of students must be made in every program. However the system is designed to provide for these functions, the design and operational decisions that must be made require a broad base of information. The development of curriculum and ongoing implementation of that curriculum in an operational program is best facilitated by ready availability of relevant information. Program management, as described in chapter 6, requires specific information to facilitate its functions. An evaluation subsystem can provide these types of information to the appropriate decision makers when needed.

Activities Necessary for Implementation

If we assume that the evaluation team is responsible for using appropriate techniques to gather and analyze most of the information needed by appropriate decision makers, it becomes apparent that program and individual performance assessment is no simple matter of gathering sporadic student opinions and recording course grades.

Across the total range of program decision areas, three kinds of assessment-related activities emerge as predominant and pervasive in the generation and analysis of data needed for program decision making: (1) assessing student performance as they demonstrate the competencies that are the terminal outcomes of competency based teacher education; (2) monitoring program operation and analyzing discrepancies found; and (3) gathering "beyond program" information.

Student-Trainee Assessment

We have established that the assessment of student-trainee performance in a competency based program is an integral part of program evaluation. It is, however, so different from student knowledge assessment in traditional teacher education programs that we shall discuss it here in some detail. As detailed in other chapters, competency based teacher education programs focus attention on teacher behavior and on the consequences of teacher behavior. Knowledge is seen as facilitating or enabling a teacher to function, i.e., to perform or behave in ways that foster pupil learning.

Although it is perfectly possible to place a high value on knowledge and therefore require a traditional demonstration of knowledge as a prerequisite to performance, this is not a necessary characteristic of competency based teacher education programs. Competency based programs place less emphasis on the demonstration of knowledge about teaching than on the performance and consequences of teaching. In this respect, student-trainee assessment takes on quite different dimensions from simple testing for knowledge acquired and stored. Whenever possible, competency should be demonstrated in terms of teacher behavior and often in terms of the consequences of that behavior.

The criteria by which teacher behavior is judged must be made explicit and means designed to assess the extent to which indicators of meeting criteria are present in a given performance. All this is perhaps best explained by an example of a teacher competency and the several levels at which the assessment is possible and/or necessary.

Consider a rather specific common diagnostic competency: "A teacher can diagnose accurately the decoding skill weaknesses of six- to eight-year-old children." There are several levels (see figure 1) at which this competency can be demonstrated. At level 1 (knowledge), given a reasonable hypothesis of the knowledge required to make such diagnoses, it is possible to construct an instrument that tests recall and application knowledge of diagnostic techniques and of the

	1	2			3				4			
	(Has demonstrated the knowledge thought to be requisite for these competencies) "Knowledge" Effectiveness Predictive Value–Low	(Has demonstrated these competencies in micro contexts) "Performance" Effectiveness Predicitive Value–Fair			(Has demonstrated these competencies in real school settings given limited responsibilities and under close supervision) "Performance" Effectiveness Predictive Value–Good				(Has demonstrated these competencies in real school settings –produces desired results with students taught) "Consequence" Effectiveness Predictive Value–High			
		Low income disadvantaged	Mixed	High	Urban Self-Contained Class	Ghetto Open Center	Suburban Self-Contained Class	Mixed Open Center	Urban Self-Contained Class	Ghetto Open Center	Suburban Self-Contained Class	Mixed Open Center
Demonstration												
Level N–K	001* 010 025 002 011 026 003 012 004 014 005 015 006 018 007 019 008 022 009 024	001(1)† 002(1)	001(2) 002(2) 003(1) 004(1) 005(2) 006(1) 008(2) 009(1) 010,etc.									
1–3							001. 002. 003. 004. 005. 009. 011. 014. 015.					
4–6			001(1) 002(2) 003(3)									

* Number refers to a specific competency.

† Number in ( ) refers to number of successful demonstrations of the competency.

Fig. 1. Elementary student/trainee competency assessment record

criteria for using the techniques. At the more realistic level 2 (performance), the teacher in training must demonstrate that he actually can make such diagnoses within acceptable accuracy limits. This, after all, is what he must do as a teacher. A competency based program will require a trainee to make such diagnoses in progressively more complex settings.

In making diagnoses, a micro context is appropriate for initial demonstration by a trainee. Here, given one or, at most, several pupils, a trainee must gather his data on the decoding skill of the pupils and make his diagnosis. Assessment at this level can be of two kinds. When the trainee is actually working with a pupil, an expert observer can evaluate the use of appropriate data-gathering techniques and can verify the diagnosis made. Accuracy of diagnosis can also be checked by providing a simulated pupil, possibly in the form of a videotape. The trainee can make a diagnosis of the taped decoding process and verify his diagnosis by checking it with a prepared diagnostic analysis. Given such taped decoding episodes, a trainee can continue to diagnose for practice and can use a self-assessment procedure to bring his competency into a successful approximation of expert judgment.

Assessment at a higher performance level (level 3 in figure 1) is reasonable to expect in a competency based program. It is not always sufficient to demonstrate competency in a micro context. Variables in real classroom settings often influence the performance capability of teachers. It is therefore appropriate to assess the same diagnostic competency in real teaching situations. This can be done either during an internship or during a short-term experience in the field, but the situational factors must be real. It is necessary, however, to provide limited time and responsibility contexts, thereby making possible a demonstration of the specific diagnostic competency in a situation that is sufficiently structured to provide assessment by a trained evaluator. In this instance, accuracy must be verified by the trained observer, who must be familiar enough with the diagnosed pupils to make such a verification and who makes his assessment based on specified criteria.

For many competencies, a higher level of assessment is possible in terms of the consequences of a teacher's performance. In the case of the diagnostic competency used in this example, there are no immediately observable consequences that can be incorporated in the assessment design. The relationship between competencies as judged by consequence criteria is discussed in a later section of this chapter.

It should be noted that the thrust in competency based teacher education to make assessments of teacher competencies at the highest possible level—i.e., at performance or consequence levels—is based on an assumption that it is more possible to predict teaching success or effectiveness by using these criteria than by using knowledge criteria alone. On the other hand, this assumption is not yet fully supported by research evidence. It has the power of logical persuasion in its favor, but it should be given high priority in teacher education research.

Cumulative Record of Competencies

Figure 1 depicts a hypothetical cumulative competency record of a sample trainee. The several levels of assessment thus become a matter of record. If we assume arbitrarily that competency 005 is the diagnostic competency described above, the record shows that the trainee has demonstrated his competencies largely with primary pupils in suburban, self-contained classroom settings. We have no evidence either from research or from this trainee's performance on which to base an effectiveness prediction beyond this type of pupil in similar situations.

However, compare the completeness of this assessment record to that of the transcript record of a student from a traditional program which shows he has received a "B" in "Reading 430" and a "Pass" in an eight-week student-teaching experience. A reasonably complete competency assessment record clearly provides considerably more information on which to base employment and further training decisions. The profile it presents can be invaluable for both purposes.

Criterion Setting: Negotiation

The criterion problem in the assessment of teacher competencies seems at first glance to be relatively straightforward. As early as the introduction, this book emphasized that in a competency based teacher education program, objectives and criteria are made as explicit as possible. It is further stated that the greatest emphasis is placed on performance or consequence criteria.

However, the process by which criteria are selected introduces considerable complexity. We agree that objectives and criteria are to be made explicit, but the issue is immediately clouded by the need to provide a degree of personalization in each trainee's instructional program. As soon as assessment moves beyond knowledge criteria to performance and consequence, the personal style that accompanies any creative teaching act and the uniqueness of every instructional context, student, or class brings into serious question any arbitrary setting of criteria by which all trainees will be judged. What works for one teacher with a given student or group of students may need to be judged somewhat differently even for the same teacher with a different student or group of students.

In a competency based program, the power to set objectives and specify criteria that every trainee must meet should not be left solely to a teacher education faculty. This power should be shared by those most centrally involved: the trainee and the practicing teacher, as well as the college faculty member. Yet programs must have some degree of control over the quality of their outcomes, and the profession needs stability and the assurance that those it certifies do possess the competencies needed to function. A process of negotiation is needed to balance these institutional demands with the demand for a program tailored to the uniqueness of each trainee.

Negotiation becomes necessary because individual student performance assessment is a very personal matter. The teacher trainee must demonstrate his competencies; this means he is being evaluated. He is obviously an active participant in the process. He is unique, with his own personal goals and style, yet he hopes to be seen as competent by his students and his colleagues. The teaching situation he faces is itself unique; every group of students is different and must be met on its particular terms. But the profession also has generalizable concerns. States, school systems, professional organizations, and college faculties may have opinions about the appropriateness and importance of certain criteria and competencies. A process of competency negotiation is feasible and necessary to facilitate mutually acceptable evaluation of teacher competencies.

In a competency based teacher education program, the evaluation subsystem must provide for regular assessment of individual trainee competencies. In practice this means that the trainee must interact regularly with program personnel charged with the assessment task. This may well be a classroom teacher and a college faculty member. Since performance with children is essential to the demonstration of many competencies, consider what each party brings to the negotiation process. The trainee brings the best awareness of his own uniqueness in terms of style, motivation, intent, and readiness. The classroom teacher brings an intimate knowledge of the assessment context, i.e., the characteristics of the particular group of students to be taught and the setting in which the performance will occur. The college faculty member brings an academic perspective and a knowledge of the criteria that have the greatest credibility with the profession at large. Through negotiation, these parties make a specific contract for performance, establish the criteria by which performance will be judged, plan the particular performance to be judged, and design the procedures to be followed in gathering and evaluating assessment data on the performance.

Other parties and other negotiation processes are possible. The negotiation process becomes a central operational feature of the evaluation subsystem. It becomes the point of intersection of the curriculum, the trainee population, and the school contexts that constitute the major field aspect of a competency based teacher education program.

Program Evaluation and Discrepancy Analysis

Provision for regular monitoring of all operational aspects of a competency based teacher education program and careful analysis of the discrepancies from design can furnish decision makers reliable information on appropriateness, affordability, and affective impact of the program.

A teacher education program must have a measure of the appropriateness of its basic goals, of each subsystem's objectives and processes, and of the basic management processes employed. Program goals and objectives must be validated against the needs of students enrolled and the profession itself. This validation can be made by submitting specified goals and objectives to the scrutiny of appropriate groups outside the program and its institution. This means that the evaluation team must develop lines of communication with persons of recognized competence representing the field of education at large. Such a group may consist of teacher educator colleagues from other institutions, representatives of public education and professional teacher groups, and representation from the populations served. The appropriateness of program goals and objectives should be assessed at least annually. The assessment information becomes an extremely useful input for the total system decision process.

Regular program monitoring involves periodic sampling of the actual operational processes of the several subsystems in a program. Each of these subsystems is designed to operate in a particular manner and to interrelate in specific ways with all of the subsystems. Periodic sampling of operational processes furnishes important information to decision makers. It should be the job of the evaluation subsystem to gather the necessary information to ascertain operational discrepancies from the original design. Again, the evaluation team makes no valuing decisions. It simply analyzes its data and reports design congruence or incongruence to management.

A program must also be perceived as relevant and satisfying to both those trained and those functioning as trainers. However, the typical intuitive assessment of the affective impact of ongoing program involvement is not adequate data for program decision making. Both students and faculty must have periodic, in some instances daily, opportunities to express their feelings about the program in which they are involved. Apart from faculty-student "rap" sessions, which may have some therapeutic value, judicious use of scaling techniques referring to specific program elements can provide a cumulative profile of the affective impact of the program. In addition, student evaluations of the learning resources can give immediate feedback regarding instructional processes. These data, along with analyses of student performance in the demonstration of competencies, provide the information needed by curriculum teams to modify instructional processes and improve the instructional program.

Such feedback requires a system capable of collecting and analyzing large quantities of data. The availability of computer facilities will to a large extent determine the amount of feedback data with which an assessment subsystem can deal. Without such capability, it is necessary to be more selective in the data collected and analyzed. Sampling procedures are in order; the frequency of collection and the size of the sample depends on the size of the program and the data management capability. The fact remains, however, that a competency based program functions best as a data based program. Every effort must be made to provide an evaluation subsystem with the capability of furnishing the data that decision makers need for design and operational decisions.

"Beyond Program" Data

As an example, if we look specifically at the decisions that must be made about recruitment, it appears that these decisions depend on "beyond program" data. More specifically, recruitment decisions should be based on information about market needs, sociocultural imperatives, and job descriptions.

The job market for teachers is not a constant within our present educational outlook. With increasing acceptance of staff differentiation, new job descriptions for emerging teacher roles are rapidly displacing descriptions of the traditional, general utility teachers. The market for teachers trained to fill these new roles must be analyzed and the results provided for recruitment policy decisions.

For instance, if information collected regularly from school teachers, administrators, college faculty, certifying authorities, and national surveys shows an emerging need for men who have the interest, commitment, and competency to serve on teaching teams working with five- and six-year-old pupils, the program decision makers must consider this data along with management inputs on available resources to determine if men can be actively recruited and how many can likely be placed in jobs when certified. In addition, community, national, and faculty inputs may suggest that, among the various sociocultural imperatives, a high priority should be assigned to encouraging blacks from economically impoverished neighborhoods to enter teaching. The recruitment policy for this emerging role may thus become one of seeking out black males to work with five- and six-year-old pupils.

Once a recruitment decision has been reached and plans made for actively recruiting, this becomes an operational activity of the program. It then becomes a responsibility of the evaluation team to monitor that activity and provide the management team with feedback that details any discrepancy between actual operation and the design for operation. Such monitoring and discrepancy analysis becomes a function of the evaluation subsystem. The discrepancy information becomes a principal tool for management to use in restructuring activities within the total system and in recommending policy and design changes.

Procedurally, the information needed for decisions on this one program area, recruitment, requires assessment techniques that go well beyond traditional educational measurement or evaluation. In this case needs assessment might take the form of sampling opinions of a stratified sample from each population comprising a data source. Polling techniques, used effectively in predicting prevailing political sentiment, should be adaptable to this process. Combined with data from more traditional state department of education and national surveys, a fairly reliable pulse of market needs can be made available.

Sociocultural imperatives can be sampled with similar techniques. However, the determination of representative samples of several data sources is a critical problem. For example, satisfactory decisions about who best represents community opinions can be arrived at only by compromise, and the samples selected must be regularly rejustified or revised to maintain credibility with all groups concerned.

The determination of job descriptions in terms of competencies required for successful performance constitutes a special case in group decision making. Public school personnel, college faculty, and, in some instances, community representatives possess unique elements of expertise to specify such competencies; each group claims the prerogative to do so. No single source should monopolize program direction. The role of the evaluation team is to gather descriptions representative of the majority opinion of a broad sample from each group and to make available any catalogued competency information.[2] However, actual descriptions of a given role must be a consensus product of decision makers representing at least school personnel, college faculty, and at times community representatives. Again, the evaluation team does not determine actual job description; it furnishes information.

Competency Assessment and Teacher Certification

Although this chapter and this book cannot explicate all the issues surrounding competency based teacher certification, there will be an obvious relationship between the activities and records of an assessment subsystem in a competency based teacher education program and the process of certifying teachers. Given a record of teacher performance assessment like the one suggested in figure 1, colleges of education, schools, and state departments of education must decide at what point a given teacher has demonstrated a sufficient repertoire and level of overall competency to merit initial certification or licensure as a teacher. It becomes a matter of the parties involved reaching agreements on the specific competencies that will be expected of all trainees, on the variation of competencies that will be allowed as teachers in training pursue their own personalized programs, on criteria by which competencies will be judged, and on the specific evidence that must be presented prior to initial certification. From an assessment standpoint, the cumulative performance information on every trainee will become the basis for decisions of many kinds, including curriculum-instruction revision, certification and employment, inservice training, and recruitment and selection. A system functions effectively and efficiently only when the information flow to all appropriate decision agents is both timely and complete. A competency based teacher education program is no exception. The central importance given to information based decision making in a competency based teacher education program demands that the system provide for the collection and analysis of many kinds of information. An evaluation subsystem can effectively provide this.

Assessment at the Consequence Level

When the consequence criterion of pupil attainment is used in assessing teaching competency, it appears that clusters of competencies yield certain pupil outcomes in synthesis performances. For instance, it may be less important to assess the trainee's ability to diagnose accurately the reading levels of six- to eight-year-old children than to assess the extent to which the teacher can bring about a specific reasonable improvement in reading skill in specific learners. This requires a synthesis of several related competencies. The test of the teacher's competencies is the consequence of his total set of behaviors; that is, do the pupils he teaches grow in the desired direction?

While continued assessment of the diagnostic competency may be less important at this level, it is important to determine the extent to which the teacher uses the diagnostic competency effectively in achieving the consequence. If the teacher is neither using his diagnostic competency nor achieving the desired consequence, the omission of the diagnostic step in the instructional process may be the basis of his failure to achieve results. Thus it becomes extremely important for the program to know which performance competencies achieve desired consequences and the extent to which trainees use those competencies in subsequent teaching assignments; *use successfully* here means use in bringing about desired consequences that are reasonable to expect of specific learners.

The requirement to update and revise the curriculum-instruction subsystem dictates extensive follow-up assessment of teachers on the job. One context in which this is most possible is the Portal School.[3] In this context, beginning teachers can cope with their initial responsibilities while still under continued training and supervision. In such schools, a major role of training personnel is the systematic collection of observational data on the performance competencies or behaviors exhibited by teachers as they cope with real instructional demands. In general, observational instruments for assessment of performance competencies in both cognitive and affective domains must yet be developed or possibly adapted from existing behavioral observation schedules.

Assuming such data are collected during the first several years of a professional's teaching career, a number of conclusions are possible, depending on the nature of the data collected. For example, programmatic problems are indicated when teachers consistently use the performance competencies they have acquired in training but do not achieve the desired consequence with their pupils. Did the institution concentrate training efforts on the wrong competencies? Is this teacher now placed in a context different from that in which he initially demonstrated his competencies? Does this signal the need for further training or for transfer to a different teaching context?

The discrepancy discovered may indicate incorrect inferences from research evidence or an inadequate research base for initial program decisions. In such instances the program must be held accountable for remediation. Program training expectancies must change and ineffective teachers must be retrained. While this stance may seem harsh today, a competency based teacher education program must accept such accountability. This clearly places immediate priorities on research to ascertain the effects of teacher behavior on pupil learning. Teacher education programs that are structured to provide the systematic assessment described in this chapter provide ideal vehicles for the conduct of this much needed instructional research.

Footnotes

1. Malcolm Provus, *Discrepancy Evaluation: For Educational Program Improvement and Assessment* (Berkeley, Calif.: McCutchan, 1972).

2. Norman Dodl, *The Florida Catalog of Teacher Competencies* (Tallahassee, Fla.: Department of Education, 1972).

3. Norman Dodl & W. Earl Armstrong, "The Portal School: Its Mission, Organization, and Implementation Problems" (available from the authors at Florida State University, Tallahassee, Fla.: May 1971).